CHINA

AND THE WTO

CHINA
AND THE WTO

Changing China, Changing World Trade

Supachai Panitchpakdi
and
Mark L. Clifford

John Wiley & Sons (Asia) Pte Ltd

This publication is designed to provide accurate and authoritative information in regard to the subject matter covered. It is sold with the understanding that the publisher is not engaged in rendering professional services. If professional advice or other expert assistance is required, the services of a competent professional person should be sought.

Other Wiley Editorial Offices

John Wiley & Sons, Inc., 605 Third Avenue, New York, NY 10158-0012, USA
John Wiley & Sons Ltd, Baffins Lane, Chichester, West Sussex PO19 1UD, England

John Wiley & Sons Australia Ltd, 33 Park Road (PO Box 1226), Milton, Queensland 4064, Australia
Wiley-VCH, Pappelallee 3, 69469 Weinheim, Germany

Library of Congress Cataloging-in-Publication Data
0-470-82061-6 (cloth)

Typeset in 11/15 points, Bembo by Linographic Services Pte Ltd
Printed in Singapore by Saik Wah Press Pte Ltd
10 9 8 7 6 5 4

Contents

Acknowledgments

This book stems from an unusual collaboration between a policy maker and a journalist; a Thai and an American. But both of us are united by our passion to see that the fruits of the extraordinary development that much of the world has seen in the past half-century are as widely distributed as possible. While much of the world enjoys riches and well-being on a scale that not even royalty could aspire to just a century ago, half of the world's population still lives on less than $2 a day. Free trade cannot solve all of the world's problems. But it is the most powerful tool that the international community has at its disposal. There is too much at stake to get development wrong. Nowhere is this truer than in China.

There are many people who contributed directly or indirectly to this book. We would like to thank Marty Carlock, Alan Choate, Jun Feng, Yongfu Gao, Fred Hu, Yiping Huang, Jean-Pierre Lehman and others who took part in the Evian Group's Forum in Hong Kong in June 2001, Mark Landler, Sean Leonard, Richard McGregor, Aida and Marilou Montajes, Tony Miller, Sam Moon, as well as Anya Schiffrin, Andy Xie and Franklyn Yao. The standard health warning applies, perhaps even more strongly in this case: none of these people endorse or are responsible for the views expressed in this book. Grateful though we are for their assistance, which made this a far better book than it would otherwise have been, any errors or misinterpretations must rest squarely upon our shoulders.

We would particularly like to thank Alysha Webb, whose research assistance made it possible to fill in many of the gaps. Mark Clifford would like to thank Steve Shepard, Bob Dowling and all of his other colleagues at *Business Week*, especially Foreign Editor Chris Power and the Hong Kong team of Frederik Balfour, Bruce Einhorn and Miguella Lam. During a decade when so much of the American media turned inward, Steve and Bob have ensured that *Business Week*'s international presence has been stronger than ever. Special thanks to Beijing Bureau Chief Tiff Roberts, who has generously shared his prodigious knowledge of China. Thanks, too, are due to the Thai WTO Mission in Geneva and the Shanghai WTO Affairs Consultation Centre. At John Wiley, Nick Wallwork and Janis Soo took this project from conception to completion with unusual speed and professionalism, aided by John Owen's skillful copy-editing.

Supachai Panitchpakdi would like to record his unbounded appreciation for the patient understanding and devotion of Sasai, Prinn and Narin, which cannot be adequately expressed in mere words.

Mark Clifford is grateful, as always, to Anya, Melissa and Ted. They were gracious in sparing me the time needed to write yet another book, far too soon after the last one.

Supachai Panitchpakdi and Mark L. Clifford
Bangkok and Hong Kong
October 2001

CHAPTER 1

China Rising

If the world needed a reminder of just how important it is to get globalization right, the September 11, 2001 terrorist attacks on the World Trade Center and the Pentagon provided a somber lesson. The assaults on the United States tragically showed the cost that people violently opposed to the affluence and freedom that are the promise of open societies can wreak. Simply ensuring that the fruits of globalization are even more abundant and are more widely shared will not alone end terrorism. But it's clearer than it has ever been that a world split between those who benefit from the increasing wealth and openness of globalization and those who don't will mean a world of increasing trouble, ranging from environmental degradation to political instability to terrorism.

Few places matter more in this debate over globalization than China. Whether it's looking out over the next few years or the next quarter-century, how the world's most populous country handles the many developmental challenges it faces will go a long way toward determining what kind of world we inhabit. Pick an issue — the environment, the military, international affairs or the global economy — and China's choices will have a major impact on Asia and the world. If China makes the wrong decisions, the result will be chilling, not only for the country's 1.3 billion citizens but for many people beyond its borders as well. Conversely, a China that successfully makes the transformation to a relatively affluent, open society will be both an inspiration to other countries and a locomotive that will help to power the world's economies.

Less than a week after the attack on the World Trade Center, China passed an important milestone in its development, one that went largely unnoticed as the world struggled to understand and respond to the terrorist threat. On September 17, in Geneva, the World Trade Organization (WTO) agreed on the final terms for the country to join the international trade body. For China, the agreement ended more than 15 years of often combative negotiations. More importantly, it confirmed a bold decision by China's leaders to lock the country into a program of broad and continuing economic reforms, reforms that should spill over into its legal system and governmental administration. The agreement signaled China's willingness to play by international trade rules and to bring its often opaque and cumbersome governmental apparatus into harmony with a world order that demands clarity and fairness.

The timing of China's WTO agreement with the attacks on New York and Washington was, of course, a coincidence. But the timing serves to highlight the battle between those who support a liberal, open world and those who would destroy it. Both the World Trade Center, where the more than 2500 victims included people from some 80 countries, and the World Trade Organization stand for an open world. That China, a country whose erratic policies often unnerved the world in the first three decades after the Communist

Party took power in 1949, has chosen to join a global rules-based organization that makes increased prosperity the heart of its mission truly is cause for celebration.

Entry into the WTO is the most significant event since China began economic reforms a quarter-century ago and ranks in importance alongside China's first nuclear weapons test in 1964.[1] WTO membership, coupled with the awarding of the 2008 Summer Olympics to Beijing in July 2001, will help China reclaim a place on the world stage that it has lost in the last two centuries. Accession to the WTO will accelerate an economic revolution that has been under way since 1978 not only in coastal cities such as Shanghai and Guangzhou but also in places like inland Chongqing and the Yangtze River towns that lie below it. WTO membership will ensure that these efforts at market reform keep powering ahead by opening up the economy to domestic and foreign competitors and firmly locking changes in place. It will help China realize its goal of doubling its gross domestic product (GDP) by 2010 and taking its place among the world's largest economies. Indeed, if China does fulfill current estimates and hit those targets, GDP would be about $2.2 trillion, slightly larger than that of Germany today. Above all, the WTO will accelerate a broad range of changes throughout Chinese society, adding fuel to a firestorm of economic and social reforms that are sweeping across China.

A strong and increasingly prosperous China will, in turn, have an enormous impact on Asia and the world. The world will have to accommodate a new economic and, perhaps, military superpower. But with WTO membership, and the entry of China into a rules-based international system, the odds are better that this new power will be one that plays by internationally accepted norms. There's no question that China's rise will be disruptive. The advent of a new regional or international power is inherently tumultuous. But the WTO is one of the most important vehicles for ensuring that this transition occurs relatively smoothly and peacefully. The existing powers made terrible mistakes a century ago when they were unsuccessful in accommodating the rise of Germany and Japan. One of the biggest mistakes at that time was to turn away from an open trading system and to retreat into ruinous protectionist policies. The result of a series of tragic miscalculations was two world wars and tens of millions of deaths. The stakes are every bit as high with China. The world needs to encourage a China that embraces openness rather than nationalism, negotiations rather than military solutions. It is virtually impossible to overstate the importance of bringing the world's most populous nation into a system that establishes internationally accepted rules for economic behavior. The value of WTO membership for China goes well beyond the business of trade.

In its simplest outlines, the WTO will set out the rules for a market-based economy. It will eliminate unfair treatment that now favors state-owned firms and discriminates against foreign companies and local entrepreneurs. By opening up protected sectors to domestic and foreign competition, from finance to agriculture, China's WTO status will ensure continued restructuring of the economy. Thousands of China's state-owned enterprises will have to reform or wither. Banks will face similar changes, changes that will be made tougher by the mountain of bad debt that's on their books, much of it a legacy of poor lending decisions to state-owned enterprises. The government will have to become more open and accountable, a big change in a culture with a longstanding and often high-handed civil service. Finally, foreign trade and direct investment is expected to increase from its already high levels.

The WTO will also have a profound effect on growth. Economists at the International Monetary Fund (IMF) estimate that, although there will be an initial period of disruption, by the time China has been in the WTO for five years its economy will grow 0.8% a year faster than it would have otherwise. That might not sound like much, but the cumulative effect of the incremental increases in growth will result in an economy that will be about $26 billion larger than it would be otherwise. With the agreed elimination of restrictions on textile exports after 2004, the impact in later years should be even greater. The IMF only looks at the impact on the Chinese economy of tariff cuts. Other studies, which also consider the impact of a lower risk premium for foreign investors, see even higher growth as a result of WTO entry.[2]

However, China's membership of the WTO could, if gloomier scenarios prove true, see a flood of imported agricultural and manufactured products inundate the entire country, which would exacerbate the already troubled situation in rural areas and in limping state-owned enterprises. In the countryside, demonstrations are increasingly common, reflecting the frustrations of farmers unhappy with stagnant incomes and rapacious local officials. Meanwhile, some 25 million of the 85 million workers at state-owned enterprises will see their jobs disappear as more-efficient foreign companies produce in China or import products from abroad. Indeed, the most pessimistic scenarios predict that the changes prompted by accession to the WTO will bring about China's collapse. Unlikely though this scenario seems, it's wise to remember that China's WTO accession is fraught with peril as well as promise.[3]

How China handles the challenges prompted by its accession to the WTO will be important. Certainly, there will be much disruption. The IMF calculates that the economy will grow 0.3% less than it would otherwise in the first year after WTO accession, a shortfall of more than $3 billion. The drop should be temporary, as reforms are instituted, but it will nonetheless be wrenching. Yet if the government uses the WTO as a spur to build modern institutions, ranging from a real legal system to a social safety net, this will usher in a modern, open economy. If, as many reformers in China hope, the WTO helps inaugurate a more rational and more market-oriented agricultural policy, the changes for China's 900 million peasants and other rural people will be every bit as profound as any in the country's 5000-year history, giving them the freedom to grow what they want and to sell it to whomever they choose. Much the same will be true for workers and business people. WTO membership is a key piece in a jigsaw puzzle of interconnected reforms and changes that are re-drawing the map of China.

Unless something goes horribly wrong, China will be one of the two or three largest economies in the world by mid-century. China's leadership is deadly serious about economic development and modernization. To understand why, and to fully appreciate why the WTO matters so much for China, it's instructive to take a detour through the turbulent years of 19th- and 20th-century China. They were times of chaos and humiliation which saw one of the world's great powers reduced to a weak state before beginning a slow climb back into the ranks of the global powers.

PRYING CHINA OPEN

For many centuries, China's developed civilization and vast population made it the world's largest economy. Indeed, as recently as 1820 China made up 28.7% of the entire world's economy (a greater share than that of the US today), well ahead of second-placed India, with its 16% share. France was a distant third, with 5.4% of the total. Back then, the US was in ninth place and had just 1.8% of the global total. The issue of how and why China squandered this pre-eminence and the best way for China to recover this lost grandeur still gnaws at the Chinese elite — its students, its academics, its dissidents and its policy makers, as well as its political leaders. For all the divisions that run through China, this desire to see the country reclaim what most Chinese see as its proper role in the world unites its people. China's pragmatic economic policies are driven by a desire to regain this former role as a great power.[4]

Imperial China boasted impressive technological achievements ranging from gunpowder to paper. Its emperors reigned over what was often the largest empire in the world — and certainly the longest-lived. A succession of eight major dynasties ruled the country over a period of 2100 years. Although the territory under imperial control waxed and waned, the Chinese state embodied threads of a unique and relatively constant culture, civilization and statecraft. No other culture can claim a record of this sort stretching back more than two millennia.

Tragically, China proved incapable of making the leap to the modern world. As the West industrialized, China proved unable to change. China's strong state had long worked to hold the vast nation together. The powerful administrative apparatus, with its brutal civil service examinations and impressive central control, had unified the country. Now, the rigidity of its system worked against growth and development. Its very strength proved too brittle to bend with the reformist winds. China's unitary system had allowed it to expand over vast tracts of territory and, unlike the short-lived empires of Alexander the Great or Genghis Khan, its strong civil service had allowed it to keep those territories through a succession of dynasties.

This centralized, homogeneous approach meant that no local power could challenge the emperor. China allowed no city-states of the sort that Europe had. There was no Magna Carta, under which the English nobles had forced their king into a modest sharing of his powers. There were none of the power-sharing arrangements between crown and town, or between king and clergy, of the sort that produced the Renaissance in Europe. The Renaissance and its intellectual ferment in turn made possible Europe's economic acceleration, first with an agricultural revolution and then an industrial revolution.

China paid as little heed to these changes as possible. The self-styled Middle Kingdom remained cocooned in its vastness. Its insularity was famously summed up by the Qianlong Emperor in 1793, when a grand and pioneering British mission headed by Lord George Macartney came to China. The British, like so many before and after, badly wanted to trade with China. Its immense untapped market was as alluring to them as it is to Coca-Cola and Procter

& Gamble today. But the mission proved to be a frustrating, stillborn one. Qianlong summed up the Chinese view, one that looked down its nose at commerce and discouraged innovation. Presented with an array of gifts designed to show off Britain's manufacturing prowess, Qianlong famously responded: "We have never valued ingenious articles, nor do we have the slightest need of your country's manufactures."[5]

The British declined to take Qianlong's refusal as the final word. They, along with other Western powers, continued agitating for more trade rights. Macau had been a Portuguese base since 1557, when the Chinese had allowed the Portuguese to set up a small base there as a reward for helping to drive away Japanese pirates. From Macau, traders could, during specified months of the year and under limited conditions laid down by the Chinese government, trade with Chinese compradors in Canton (today's Guangzhou). The British joined the Portuguese and other foreign traders in establishing commercial ties with the Chinese using these southern ports.

But the British kept itching for more. Push came to shove in a series of small conflicts popularly known as the Opium Wars, which took their name from one of the most profitable goods that Britain was determined to sell — and which the Chinese were determined to keep out. In 1842, China ceded the island of Hong Kong, at the mouth of the Pearl River delta, as part of the price of defeat in this conflict that was fought as Britain struggled to win commercial and trading rights with China. Britain's success prompted other countries to press for their own concessions. By the end of the century China was carved up by foreign powers. Few major cities were untouched by a significant foreign presence, often one that manifested itself in a socially segregated foreign compound.

A series of treaties forced on China by gunboat diplomacy gave the British, French, Germans, Japanese and Russians extraordinary privileges. Among these were a number of so-called treaty ports, enclaves that the foreigners ruled as colonies. Although Hong Kong was the first of these, Shanghai was, until 1949, the most prominent. The enclaves were an important concession. But foreign immunity from Chinese courts was even more important. Because foreign countries didn't trust China's often capricious and brutal legal system, they demanded and won the right to be immune from trial in Chinese courts — an extraordinary loss of sovereignty for China. The treaties also gave foreign powers the right to set tariffs — and to collect them. Besides the Customs Service, foreigners controlled China's lighthouses, pilot boats and the postal system. China's modern economy was a foreign business. British trading houses such as Butterfield & Swire and Jardine Matheson dominated many of these enclaves. Foreign banks, such as the Hong Kong and Shanghai Bank, controlled finance. The late 19th century nationalist Kang Youwei understandably complained that his country was being sliced up "like a melon".

Even today, the Chinese rightly refer to these documents forced on them as the Unequal Treaties. The scars that they left shouldn't be ignored. It's sometimes easy to dismiss the suspicion, even hostility, with which many Chinese regard opening to the outside world and the changes wrought by the world trading system. Considering that this was a country that had no desire to trade with the outside world two centuries ago, the eagerness with which

China has embraced world trade in the last quarter-century is surprising. After all, the country was pried open by force, subjected to humiliating treaties that allowed foreigners unprecedented privileges, and remained prostrate for most of the intervening decades. The state media stokes some of this sense of wounded nationalism, much to the annoyance of foreigners, but these strident nationalist calls touch a powerful chord for understandable reasons. Even the country's Western-educated elite is determined to resist their country ever again being the plaything of stronger foreign powers.

Japan faced similar pressure from the West to open its doors to trade in the mid-19th century. After some hesitation, it successfully embraced economic modernization following the 1868 Meiji Restoration. China, like its tributary state Korea, proved unable to make the transition. A series of timid reforms in the late 19th century produced little result. China's humiliation increased with the 1899–1900 Boxer Rebellion. Nationalists failed in their determination to drive foreigners out of China, but not before killing hundreds of British, Americans and other Westerners. To avenge the killings, armies from the foreign powers invaded and this eight-nation incursion onto Chinese soil marked yet another stage in the humbling of China. The country's crumbling economy sagged further under the weight of a massive indemnity that the invading forces negotiated as part of the compensation for the losses they had suffered during the Boxer Rebellion. Little more than a decade later, in 1911, the Qing dynasty fell. China's imperial age was at an end.

The collapse of the imperial order left a vacuum that the newly founded Republic of China failed to fill. The following years were a time of conflict and chaos. China's most prominent anti-Qing nationalist, Sun Yat-sen, proved unable to lead effectively. A succession of warlords and revolutionaries fought for control. Foreign powers continued to prey on China's weakness. Japan's invasion of the northeastern province of Manchuria presaged a further slicing up of the country. But China's two main contenders for power, Chiang Kai-shek's Kuomintang (KMT) and Mao Zedong's Chinese Communist Party, proved unable to unite effectively. World War II provided some respite in the struggle between the KMT and the Communists. But when the international conflict was over, the two sides resumed their civil war. Despite US support, Chiang's KMT was forced to retreat to Taiwan in defeat. China's traditional territorial integrity was largely restored, with the glaring exceptions of Taiwan, Hong Kong and Macau. No longer would it be sliced up like a melon. But it was impoverished, devastated and exhausted by war.

COME THE REVOLUTION

On October 1, 1949, the victorious peasant-turned-revolutionary Mao Zedong stood atop the rostrum in front of Beijing's Forbidden City and proclaimed that "China has stood up". Under Mao and Communist rule, China cleansed itself of foreign influence, realizing much of the nationalist agenda. But the cost of this anti-foreign salve set China back even further economically. The communists drove all foreign businesses and almost all foreigners out of Shanghai and the other treaty ports that had been such a humiliation for the previous century. China had been Coca-Cola's largest market outside of the United States, the first country abroad where the soft-drink company sold a million cases in a single year. But soon after the revolution Coke shut up shop in China, not to return for more than three decades. Many Chinese left as well. Streams of Shanghai's Chinese elite fled to Hong Kong, providing a needed boost for the British colony but eviscerating what had been Asia's most cosmopolitan commercial center.

Mao embarked on a period of radical agricultural reform. By 1956, agriculture had been collectivized. Except for the smallest kitchen gardens, private farming was abolished everywhere except Tibet. Something like two million landlords paid with their lives as this policy was implemented. Productivity shot up in the first years of land reform, which gave land back to the peasants. But the advent of collectives didn't lead to the grain surpluses that Mao had envisaged.

Next came the Great Leap Forward of 1958–60, which resulted from Mao's impatience with agricultural reform and his desire to jump-start development. In the end, it was a giant step backward, an era whose collective madness presaged the Cultural Revolution. Pots and pans were melted down to provide raw material for backyard steel furnaces that produced worthless metal. Sparrows, regarded as pests, were hunted close to extinction. When Defense Minister Peng Dehuai dared question the policy in 1959 he was purged, leading to the first major split in the Chinese Communist Party. A famine that resulted in part from these mad policies killed perhaps 30 million people.

Even after the disastrous Great Leap, Mao chafed at what he saw as the increasing bureaucratization of his revolution. His response was the 1966 launch of the Cultural Revolution, a movement that proved every bit as tragic and devastating as the Great Leap Forward. The Cultural

Revolution saw, by official Chinese accounts, 100 million people "treated unjustly".[6] Deng Xiaoping, one of the top people in the Party hierarchy, was just one of many members of the elite sent to work on a farm. Students attacked teachers, a new low in a country that revered learning and scholarship. Then universities were shut. "Class enemies" were paraded in dunces' caps. Government largely broke down in parts of the country. Radical organizations at the local level fought each other for power. Priceless cultural artifacts were destroyed by youthful Red Guards intent on sweeping away the remnants of the old Confucian order. Every action, even private disputes between husband and wife, was politicized and examined in the light of class struggles and Maoist precepts.

The revolution was in danger of consuming itself. Mao and his ultra-leftist allies in the Gang of Four attacked President Liu Shaoqi, a longtime communist and second only to Mao in the Party hierarchy. Mao opposed Liu's use of material incentives to increase agricultural production. As Liu struggled to keep the impact of the Cultural Revolution within bounds, he fell victim to the madness that swept the country. Dismissed from his posts in 1968, derided as "a renegade, a traitor and a scab", Liu was tortured, imprisoned and died in jail in 1969. If further proof was needed that the revolution was devouring itself, the death of Lin Biao in a 1971 plane crash provided it. Lin, at the time Mao's number two, had apparently been plotting to assassinate the chairman and seize power.

The political upheavals of Mao's time continue to matter. They helped instill in every Chinese who lived through them a deep fear of chaos, or what the Chinese call *luan*, and an instinctive desire for stability. The government has been able to play on that fear to justify its heavy-handed grip on the country. That's been especially true since the collapse of communism in Eastern Europe and the former Soviet Union in the late 1980s and early 1990s. It continues today, as senior communist leaders warn of the chaos that would result if China went the way of the former USSR or Yugoslavia or Indonesia. For a people who have seen a century of chaos, it's an argument that finds a receptive audience. It remains to be seen if a younger populace, one that grew up in the relative affluence of the post-1978 period and is largely the product of single-child families, will feel the same fear of change.

Economically, Mao's legacy was a sorry one indeed. He had talked of economic development, but China slid further back during his impetuous, tumultuous reign. By 1978 China accounted for barely 7% of the world economy, compared with more than one-quarter a century-and-a-half earlier. China would now race to make up for lost time.

RIDING THE REFORM TIGER

It fell to a short, stout, round-faced peasant to unleash the next, greatest Chinese revolution. Deng Xiaoping was a longtime communist cadre born to a wealthy landlord in Sichuan province, not far from the banks of the Yangtze River. He studied in Paris and Moscow before returning to China. A veteran organizer of peasant rebellions and a participant in Mao's legendary Long March during the Chinese civil war, Deng emerged after the revolution as a senior communist leader. In 1956 he was named General Secretary of the Party. While Mao could be an often erratic, romantic revolutionary, Deng was pragmatic. He locked horns with Mao over the futility of the Great Leap Forward. During the Cultural Revolution he was purged and sent to work on a pig farm. His son, Deng Pufang, jumped, or was thrown by tormentors, from a Beijing building during the Cultural Revolution and has been confined to a wheelchair ever since. Deng knew firsthand the human and national cost of Mao's revolutionary excesses.

Deng moved quickly to consolidate power after Mao's death in 1976. Two years later, he announced the first of a series of increasingly bold economic reforms. He began by instituting the household responsibility system, which gave individual farmers responsibility for their own small plots of land. After meeting a state quota, farmers could sell the rest of what they produced on the open market. The system was aimed at doing away with the vast, low-productivity agricultural communes that accounted for much of the country's crop production. By giving land back to the peasants, Deng unleashed a productivity surge that provided bumper crops. That freed up labor for other enterprises and saw farmers drop as a percentage of the workforce from 71% in 1978 to 50% in 1995.

From the time Deng's reforms started in 1978 until the mid-1990s, about 200 million people were lifted out of poverty, a number almost as large as the entire population of the United States at the time the reforms began. Per capita incomes quadrupled, and farmers and city dwellers alike began to buy goods that they previously could only dream of. Televisions were a luxury when Deng's reforms started. By the time he died almost two decades after launching his reforms, the telltale luminescent flicker of the television set was found in most of the country's households. Foreign direct investment also surged as a result of Deng's decision to once again open China to the world. By the time of Deng's death in 1997, China was sucking in $40 billion a year in foreign direct investment, a figure second only to the United States.

The changes led to a roller-coaster Chinese economy. Inflation accelerated in the late 1980s as controls on many prices were lifted and investment surged. Then the government slammed on the brakes. The economy flagged amidst an austerity program and gloom among foreign investors that followed the brutal crackdown on the 1989 Tiananmen Square democracy protests. By the early 1990s, the future of economic reform looked very much in doubt. In 1992, at the age of 87, in his last significant public act, Deng toured the southern Special Economic Zone of Shenzhen, a boom town that bordered Hong Kong. He urged his compatriots to speed up economic growth and to push ahead with economic reform and foreign investment. Although Deng had retired from all of his prestigious positions, he remained the paramount leader. Deng's southern tour jolted China and set off a new round of growth unlike anything the country had ever seen, topping 12% for several years running.

Even allowing for the suspicion shared by many analysts that China overstates its growth numbers, the figures from these years are staggering. In 1992, with the country electrified by Deng's call to speed up reform, the economy expanded 14.2%. The next year it grew 13.5% and in 1994 growth was another 12.7%. Even in 1995, as central bank governor Zhu Rongji tried to put the brakes on, growth only dropped to 10.5%. It was also in the early 1990s that Shanghai re-opened its stock exchange. The country's other major stock exchange, in Shenzhen, opened during this same period. Shenzhen saw rioting in August 1992 when tens of thousands of people stampeded to the exchange in hopes of getting application forms for initial public stock offerings. Until the 1990s, there was the possibility that China could turn its back on economic reform. Deng had to fight many old Party cadres who opposed the pragmatic, market-friendly economic revolution he spearheaded.

By the time of Deng's death, the economy had changed almost beyond recognition. Economic growth from 1978 to 2000 averaged 9% annually, an extraordinary record that tops the global records established by South Korea and Taiwan — in a country whose population totals 20 times that of these two dragons combined. And it far outstripped the performance of the Western powers at the time they humiliated China during the 19th century. Britain grew about 1.2% annually from 1830 to 1910, during the heyday of its industrial revolution. In two decades, notes the World Bank, China "has accomplished what took other nations centuries".[7]

One of Deng's greatest legacies, perhaps an inadvertent one, was to leave China firmly in the hands of a chosen successor, Jiang Zemin. Jiang vaulted to the position of the Communist Party General Secretary in the turmoil that followed the suppression of the 1989 protests. Few expected him to be more than a transitional figure. They pointed to the fact that Deng's previous anointed heir, Hu Yaobang, had been shunted unceremoniously aside in 1987. Deng himself had emerged at the top of the ruling elite only after pushing aside Mao's chosen heir, Hua Guofeng. But because Deng was enfeebled in his final years, Jiang had a window of opportunity during which his patron was alive but unable to intervene except in the most critical decisions.

That allowed Jiang to establish his authority and legitimacy and thus to confound the doubters and beat the odds against a smooth transfer of power in a one-party state.

Yet this cautious and seemingly unremarkable man has presided over a period of extended growth and tranquility. One of Jiang's most significant moves was to bring one of his colleagues from Shanghai, where Jiang had been Party Secretary, to Beijing. He made former Shanghai mayor Zhu Rongji vice-premier. Zhu, who quickly assumed the position of central bank governor and in 1998 became premier, proved himself to be among the most adroit economic managers in Chinese history. First, in 1994 he stepped on the economic brakes to slow an economy that was spiraling into hyperinflation, with consumer prices rising more than 20% annually. For the first time in modern China, Zhu succeeded in engineering a soft economic landing, bringing growth down from 12.7% in 1994 to 7.8% by 1998. Then, to fight spreading deflation caused by the economic slowdown and a glut of production, he adopted a far-reaching stimulus program, with heavy spending on much-needed infrastructure and housing.

In 1997, at a Communist Party Congress (a major event held only once every five years), Jiang proclaimed a sweeping reform of state-owned enterprises. That announcement, along with the Asian financial crisis, spurred a new round of economic reforms that saw China inch toward privatization of many of its state-owned enterprises. Private property rights were enshrined in the constitution two years later, in August 1999. Zhu's stimulus program spawned a private housing market. That policy, coupled with a burgeoning private sector, freed large numbers of people from the shackles of the *danwei* system. From the early days of the revolution, the *danwei*, or work units, had controlled where people worked and where they lived and, for many years, had even distributed food. For millions of workers, the changes meant that local Party functionaries would no longer decide how large an apartment they enjoyed or what job they could take.

Human-rights advocates complain about the absence of explicitly political rights and the ruthlessness with which the government acts against its opponents. Arguably, China had more political freedom in the late 1980s than it has enjoyed at any time since the June 1989 crackdown on pro-democracy protestors. At that time, almost no one would have imagined the extraordinary economic events that took place in the 1990s. Nor would they have imagined how little the political and human-rights situation would change. But, thanks largely to economic reform, more Chinese enjoy more personal freedom and are more affluent than at any time in history. There is a growing middle class and a diversity of views and interests of a sort that China has rarely seen before. A "rights culture" has developed, as increasingly assertive consumers and others use the courts to protect their interests. It's impossible to say that China is as pluralistic as, say, Taiwan or Korea, but its affluent urban pockets are much closer to those two neighbors than to the austere, totalitarian China of the 1960s and 1970s.

But there is far to go. With WTO entry, China is simply at the end of the beginning of reform. Like many developing nations, China's leaders for decades confused economic development with smokestack industries. State plans channeled money and other scarce resources to heavy industries such as steel and chemicals. But these capital-intensive industries were notoriously inefficient. As China reformed its economy, one of the biggest challenges was how to turn the state-owned enterprises into modern businesses. During the mid-1990s, China flirted with the idea of establishing Korean-style industrial groups, hoping to turn its lumbering giants into something like Seoul's *chaebol*. Indeed, a team of experts from Beijing had already booked their plane tickets for a study mission to Seoul in 1997 when the Asian economic crisis hit. Fortunately for China, Korea's financial troubles, which resulted in a record $58 billion bailout by the IMF and the collapse of many of the *chaebol*, convinced the Chinese of that model's folly.

Instead, China has embarked on a far more promising road to reform by listing shares of some of its biggest companies on the New York and Hong Kong stock exchanges. The April 2000 initial public offering of petroleum giant PetroChina, which raised $3.9 billion for 10% of the shares of the world's fourth-largest petroleum company, marked a milestone for China. PetroChina was formed by hiving off the exploration, production and refining units of China National Petroleum Corporation (CNPC) and leaving the rump with the parent company. The split saw 480,000 people join the new company, while 1,020,000 people who worked in ancillary parts of the giant petroleum company — teachers, nurses, maintenance people — remained behind at CNPC.

Measured by stock-market capitalization or production, PetroChina ranks among the half-dozen largest oil companies in the world. The overseas stock listing means that it must meet international financial and disclosure norms. While its financial performance and its corporate-governance standards are a long way from giants like

ExxonMobil, Shell and BP, it is nonetheless a remarkable transformation for one of China's giant state-owned companies. Refiner China Petroleum & Chemical Corporation (Sinopec), a similarly large and unwieldy state-owned enterprise, followed a few months after PetroChina with an initial public offering that raised more than $4 billion. In early 2001, China National Offshore Oil Corporation also listed its shares in New York and Hong Kong. China's two largest mobile telecommunications companies have also listed overseas. The fact that some of the country's biggest enterprises have gone from being part of government ministries in a planned economy to Wall Street-listed firms reflects the extraordinary changes in the last two decades. Listings like these won't be a panacea for the many ills that ail Chinese corporations, but the international oversight they bring at least holds out the possibility of pushing corporate reform forward.

Meanwhile, the domestic economy has changed almost beyond recognition. The private sector now accounts for most economic output, as we will discuss in detail in Chapter 5. This has helped China make the transition from a scarcity economy to one of surpluses. Items that were luxuries at the beginning of the 1990s, from televisions to automobiles to airline tickets, have seen fierce price competition as a flood of investment has brought vast new capacity onto the market. Unsuccessful government-sponsored attempts to fix minimum prices or limit production have only succeeded in illustrating how successful economic reform has been. The deflation that has resulted from the explosion in manufacturing production has been ruinous to many producers but a boon to consumers.

In all, this has been an extraordinary time. In the nearly quarter-century since economic reform began, China has gone from a hermetic nation of drably dressed people in a planned, state-led economy to the world's seventh-largest economy today, with its $1.1 trillion in annual output ranking second only to Japan in Asia.

The macroeconomic reforms driving change are simple. A high savings rate provided enough investment capital to fuel growth, even though many of these investments were wasted on low- or no-return projects. Macroeconomic stability was high, at least by developing-country standards, and government policy provided enough certainty for businesses, consumers and foreign investors to make increasingly market-driven decisions. A productive labor force also played an important role. China's workers are, by comparison with their peers in developing countries, efficient and well-organized, reflecting both a disciplined (some might say punitive or unduly deferential) culture and relatively high levels of education. Finally, a strong, effective and pragmatic state dedicated to high economic growth proved necessary to translate the desire for economic development into reality.

AGENDA FOR REFORM

Much of the revolution that Deng Xiaoping unleashed simply represented a catch-up from the lost decades of the post-1949 period. Tremendous reforms have been accomplished and much of the groundwork for a more modern China has been laïd. But many of the most difficult reforms still lie ahead. The WTO will ensure that the momentum for change continues, even in the face of internal resistance. The financial sector needs to be overhauled so that capital flows to productive areas rather than serving political or government imperatives. Reform of the troubled state-owned enterprise sector must continue. These massive companies employ about 85 million people in all, so any restructuring needs to be done in a way that takes account of the social cost of reform.

Even bigger reforms loom on the institutional side. Legal reform is indispensable for the development of a modern economy. Without property rights that are firmly rooted in laws that people can rely on, economic growth will suffer. As it is, both foreign and domestic businesses complain of the opaque, even corrupt, manner in which many decisions are made in China and the deterrent effect that this has on investments. The culture of connections, of *guanxi*, must give way to one of laws. In a society where *guanxi* has mattered for centuries, that will be a wrenching transformation. Will local officials cede their power to the courts? Will the Communist Party?

Singapore provides an interesting example of an open economy and a closed political system, where the legal system is regarded as free of taint in commercial matters yet the government has maintained tight political control, in large part with an aggressive use of the law. Hong Kong, which now lies within China's borders, has a fair and objective legal system that Beijing has largely left untouched. Yet even though China's leaders say they want to develop a law-based society, it's not simply a matter of mimicking these former colonies, which use a variant of the British common-law legal tradition developed during more than a century of colonial rule. China has a very different legal tradition, as well as a philosophy that sees law as an instrument of rule.

In agriculture, which has seen sweeping reform, much remains to be done. China needs to push ahead with plans to lease land for longer periods so that farmers have an incentive to invest in higher value-added fruit crops, for example, which usually require more investment and longer gestation periods. There are specific reforms, such as the end of the grain-procurement system, which forces farmers to grow grain rather than more profitable crops, that should be adopted. But peasants, like everyone else in the country, need above all to know that they won't be squeezed by local officials or disadvantaged by capricious government policies. To do that, law must be on their side.

& & &

Inequality is on the rise in China. Urban workers' earnings are more than double those of their rural counterparts and the gap is growing. So, too, is the divide between the relatively well-off coastal provinces and the impoverished interior. Although the number of absolute poor dropped by about 200 million people during the first two decades of reform, there are still 70 million people living in absolute poverty. Another 100 million are living on less than $1 a day, deriving almost half of their paltry incomes selling grain they grow. Government procurement policies, which artificially depress the price of grain, hurt these people. WTO requirements will have a double-edged effect. On one side, they will push reform faster, because the government will be under pressure to respond to the challenge of cheaper imported food. A more market-oriented agricultural policy would help. Letting farmers grow more profitable cash crops, rather than forcing them to grow grain, would also benefit the poor. So, too, would permission to leave the countryside in search of work in towns and cities. Rural incomes could be raised by eliminating many of the distortions in the agricultural market. But WTO entry could turn farmers against reform if their situation deteriorates further.

Urban poverty isn't yet a major issue. But 25 million workers have been laid off from state-owned enterprises since 1997 and the jobs of many of the 85 million who remain are at risk. Many workers, especially in towns and cities with a single state-owned enterprise dominating the economy, are unlikely to be able to find new jobs. For these workers above all, China needs to ensure that promised pension benefits are paid. Too often, local companies or local authorities are unable or unwilling to pay benefits due to workers. This has fueled demonstrations in some locations, especially when corrupt or inept managers have squandered funds. China has a pay-as-you-go pension system. Its liabilities exceed its assets by nearly $100 billion. A good deal of the shortfall can be filled by selling off state shares, but this will require prompt, decisive action in order to forestall a full-blown crisis prompted by the country's aging population.

❧   ❧   ❧

By virtue of its large size and rapid growth, China is fast becoming an environmental nightmare. For the sake of the Chinese people, as well as for the world, it is imperative that China move firmly and steadily to prevent further environmental degradation. Already, China has many of the world's most polluted cities. The World Bank estimates that as many as 289,000 deaths a year in China could be avoided if air pollution levels simply were reduced to meet existing Chinese legal standards. In all, the Bank estimates that the economic costs of the country's air and water pollution equal 3–8% of annual GNP.[8] Pollution tends to rise with economic development, then fall as countries become richer and citizens demand a cleaner environment. The World Bank calculates that deepening reforms can ensure that China doesn't follow this classic "get dirty, get rich, get clean" strategy.

The Bank points to two primary environmental culprits: coal and urbanization. Coal accounts for 80% of China's energy needs. Much of it is high-sulfur, polluting coal. And much of it is used inefficiently, in homes and apartments and small-scale industrial boilers. Death rates for chronic obstructive pulmonary disease are five times as high in China as in the United States. Some of this is due to higher smoking rates. But much of it is due to higher indoor and outdoor pollution levels. Besides higher death rates, the Bank estimates that pollution results in 11 million emergency-room visits and 566,000 hospital admissions a year. That puts a further strain on China's overburdened health-care system.

What does any of this have to do with economic reform, let alone the WTO? Economic reform can bring about more market-oriented policies that would encourage more energy efficiency. Adopting the principle that polluters should pay the economic cost of their actions would force many companies and individuals to change their behavior dramatically, at a relatively low overall cost to the country. Although coal prices in coastal regions are now near world market prices, the use of high-sulfur coal is not penalized. So there is little incentive to use cleaner coal. Gasoline prices are also low by international standards, meaning there is little reason to use more efficient engines. Interestingly, economic reforms may already be having an effect on pollution control efforts. Some of the most polluting companies are old-line state-owned industries. As reforms squeeze their operations, they are slowly being replaced by newer, cleaner competitors. Poor countries and poor people have a disproportionately large impact on the environment. Planned economies are among the worst polluters, because they pay little attention to costs, as the former Soviet Union so tragically demonstrated.

Urbanization presents another big environmental hurdle. Because China has had an effective planning system, the overly rapid urbanization that has been the bane of many developing countries has been avoided so far. Still, between 1978 and 1995 the official population of China's cities swelled by 180 million people. In addition, perhaps another 50 million unauthorized residents moved from the countryside to cities, making up a seemingly inexhaustible pool of labor that kept wages low in China's export factories. With the weakening *hukou* system, which limits the movement of rural workers into cities, it's imperative that China's leaders adopt environmentally sustainable urban policies before the tide of rural–urban immigration gets larger. One area to watch is policies for the automobile industry. Chinese leaders dropped automobiles in favor of housing in their list of pillar industries in the late 1990s, implicitly recognizing that rapid development of the automobile sector would be an environmental nightmare. With foreign auto makers gearing up to take advantage of WTO arrangements, it will be a test of China's development policy to manage increased numbers of vehicles.

In addition to the big problems of coal use and urbanization, China faces a slew of other environmental challenges. Deforestation and development have worsened the periodic floods faced by the country's farmers. A chronic water shortage in the northern part of the country threatens continued economic development. Many workers' health remains under threat from poor working conditions. Neither the WTO nor a market economy will by themselves solve these problems. But by bringing more transparency and more of a market orientation to environmental issues, they lay the way toward ending the worst abuses and helping ensure that China doesn't follow the classic strategy of worrying about pollution only after the country has developed. That would be ruinous not only to China and its people but to the entire region.

≈   ≈   ≈

One of China's biggest obstacles is institutional. This is where China's entry into the WTO becomes most uncertain. Better institutions of all sorts — from courts to the police force to corporate boards — are indispensable in cementing economic reform in China. If peasants don't have some certainty that the land they farm is going to be theirs for the next 30 or 60 years, they won't invest in improving it. If entrepreneurs don't know that courts and the government will set out and enforce clear rules and protect their rights, China will have more get-rich-quick schemers and fewer socially beneficial investors who build enduring companies that create jobs and profits and pay the taxes needed for a government whose revenue base is alarmingly fragile.

Without these sorts of well-run and transparent companies, foreign investment and trade will remain more limited.

Indeed, one of the greatest lessons of the Asian crisis of the late 1990s is that institutional structures are a prerequisite for sustained economic growth. Certainly, growth can flourish in countries with poor institutional underpinnings during good times. But the importance of strong institutional foundations becomes clear when economic storms rage. The ability of Hong Kong and Singapore to emerge from the Asian financial turmoil relatively unscathed reflects, above all, good governance and good macroeconomic policy. By and large, banks in both places base their lending on commercial decisions rather than political connections or under-the-table payments. Courts and regulators in Hong Kong and Singapore are arguably the most effective in Asia in protecting the rights of minority shareholders, in contrast to corrupt and incompetent judicial systems in many other countries in the region. China has made a start on institutional reform. The China Securities Regulatory Commission, which regulates the stock market, enjoys broad regulatory power. It has brought in foreign experts, including the former vice-chair of Hong Kong's Securities and Futures Commission, to try to institute better standards. Chinese judges are studying the experience of Hong Kong to prepare for entry into the WTO and Hong Kong legal experts are training their counterparts across the border.

Make no mistake: despite far-reaching reforms, the Communist Party remains the primary power in China. There is no independent judiciary. Indeed, the courts rank as no more powerful than a ministry. They have little power to enforce their decisions. Although the educational level of judges has been improving, many judges are ill-educated. During the 1980s, it was common for the state to assign People's Liberation Army soldiers who had been decommissioned to become judges. Not surprisingly, many of them saw their job as protecting the state, rather than trying to enforce rules even-handedly — which might, in some cases, have meant protecting citizens *from* the state.

China has a tradition of using laws to punish citizens rather than to provide a neutral arbiter of rules. Discretionary power, from the emperor to petty officials, was large. Relationships often mattered more than rules. China's capricious legal system was the reason that foreigners pushed for the right to be exempt from the Chinese legal system. Legal reform began during the last years of the Qing dynasty. But even during the best of times, it was more the ideal than the reality.

The Communist Party's revolutionary victory in 1949 did away with even the ideal of an independent legal system. The Party was the supreme authority. And because the interests of the state and of the people were supposed to be the same, there wasn't any need to have an independent referee to adjudicate disputes. The tragic follies of Mao's years showed the dangers of not having an independent check on power. After Mao's death, dissidents during the 1978–79 Democracy Wall movement (notably Wei Jingsheng) pushed for legal reforms as part of broader democratic reform. More recently, President Jiang Zemin has talked repeatedly about the need to establish rule of law. Yet, it's unclear whether Chinese officials really want rule *of* law or rule *by* law. Tellingly, lawyers are still occasionally imprisoned for doing nothing more than protecting their clients' rights.

The National People's Congress has become far livelier in the past two decades. Although it's not the rubber stamp that it was in the 1980s and before, it's still a long way from being an independent center of power. Perhaps its most incandescent moment, in terms of a possible role as an independent institution, came in 1992 when more than one-third of delegates voted against the massive Three Gorges Dam project. Still, it wasn't enough to stop the dam from going ahead and, so far, it hasn't heralded a larger role for the Congress.

WHY WTO MEMBERSHIP MATTERS FOR CHINA

In Shanghai, a huge sign with the letters "WTO" — a blood-red, sword-shaped "T" severs the "W" and the "O" — dominates a corner of Huaihai Road, one of China's busiest shopping areas. Along with the 2008 Beijing Olympics, WTO status will mark China's arrival on the world scene as emphatically as its emergence as a nuclear power did in 1964. Already, the WTO has taken on almost mythic importance in China. Although there are proper Chinese characters to describe the organization, they're usually ignored. Instead, the three English letters "WTO" are scattered through newspapers and bandied about on television and the radio. In the run-up to WTO accession, China fixated on what membership would mean. Newspapers carried editorials on it almost every day. Even taxi drivers were well-versed in WTO lingo. More than 50 books on the subject were published in the past few years, ranging from academic tomes to simple explanations of what WTO entry means for the average Chinese person.

But there's a lot more than the strutting of a would-be superpower at work here. After nearly a quarter-century of cautious, experimental reforms, China is getting to the truly hard part of transforming its economy. Some big issues, such as legal and governmental reform, must be pushed forward. So must a myriad of micro-reforms, ones that affect individual industries. These are precisely the sorts of reforms that will attract opposition from interests with the most to lose. Jiang Zemin and Zhu Rongji recognize that WTO membership will lock in reforms and guard against backsliding in a range of areas from tariff levels to competition policy to government procurement. The requirements of WTO membership will also accelerate reforms by forcing China to do more than it might otherwise do. It will be harder for domestic opponents to fight changes that are required to bring the country into compliance with WTO regulations. Because the WTO mandates lower tariffs, fewer barriers to competition and a more transparent regime, needed reforms will be pushed to a new level. That should ensure high growth and continued economic gains. As it is, the present mix of a command economy and a market economy is confusing and is as likely to hinder growth as to promote it. After all, a world of five-year plans and government decisions will be increasingly ineffective as the economy grows in complexity and size.

The benefits of an open China that is integrated into the world economy, an integration that is anchored by WTO membership, are extraordinary. The World Bank estimates that, if international economic engagement and opening go ahead as planned, China's share of world trade will more than triple, to 10%, by 2020, as it imports vastly increased quantities of everything from rice to semi-conductor equipment. At the same time, its exports will grow dramatically as it accounts for a growing share of the world's production of labor-intensive export products. According to these estimates, China will be the world's second-largest trading nation, with its 10% share of world exports trailing only the United States (which will have 12%) and putting it well ahead of Japan (which will have an estimated 5% of global exports). China will account for a full 40% of the estimated increase in imports by developing countries.[9]

If the World Bank's optimistic scenario of 7% compounded annual economic growth plays out, China's share of world economic output will rise from 1% in 1992 to nearly 4% in 2020. This figure uses nominal exchange rates. Many economists prefer to use another method of economic measurement, known as purchasing-power parity, to try to account for very different prices in high-income and low-income countries. Using this yardstick, China would become the world's second-largest economy in 2020, with 8% of global output. It would trail only the United States, which would account for 19% of the global economy using this measure.

China's workers would be big beneficiaries. The World Bank estimates that wages for China's unskilled workers would lead the global growth pack, increasing almost three-and-a-half times from 1992 to 2020. China's skilled workers would also see the world's highest wage gains among skilled workers, with nearly a doubling during the period. If this comes to pass, it would be an extraordinary phenomenon. Amidst the concern over China's labor policies, especially on the part of labor unions and consumers in the rich world, it's worth underscoring just how much Chinese workers have to gain from increased trade.

WTO membership will also ensure that China doesn't follow the more autarkic policies that Japan and Korea pursued. These export-oriented, heavy-industry policies paid tremendous dividends for both Korea and Japan. But they carried heavy costs, both domestically and internationally. Domestically, they resulted in companies that were protected from competition and thus made large mistakes, mistakes that have cost taxpayers of both countries dearly as they have paid to bail out banks that made ill-advised lending decisions to failed companies. Internationally, the massive export pushes of these countries led to conflict with trading partners. China's size means that international trading partners would be even more concerned about the development of an export juggernaut that restricted imports into the Chinese market than they were in the case of Japan and Korea.

The WTO and its pro-competition policies should ensure that China doesn't succumb to the temptation to pursue policies too obviously favoring the growth of big-business groups and the adoption of protectionist policies. Similarly, in agriculture WTO membership should make it impossible for China to pursue policies designed to protect grossly inefficient farmers. However costly protecting farmers might be for long-term economic development, it's something that both Japan and South Korea did for domestic political reasons. By spurring economic growth, being part of the WTO should help China create the jobs to absorb its labor surplus.

There now is virtually no danger of a leftist, anti-market domestic challenge to reforms, unlike the situation that prevailed as recently as a decade ago. Rather, the danger now is that a crony-style capitalism develops and that China's economic reforms are stillborn. The experiences of the former Soviet Union and of Indonesia show, in very different ways, what can happen if proper institutional frameworks aren't built. By reducing discretionary power and promoting transparency, WTO status should help whittle away at corruption. Just as central authorities are using listings of major state-owned companies on the New York and Hong Kong stock exchanges to help improve governance, WTO membership will mean a more law- and rule-oriented society throughout the country. By establishing fair, open rules, domestic entrepreneurs will have a better chance of competing against state-owned companies. New entrants will be able to fight back against arbitrary policies laid down by local officials intent on protecting hometown companies or cronies.

Chinese domestic companies will be some of the biggest beneficiaries. Right now they have to deal with local protectionism. They find it hard to resist rapacious local officials. They are often at a disadvantage even in competing with foreign companies, who get tax breaks and other preferential treatment. "This is an historic opportunity for China's private economy," says Liu Yonghao, head of the New Hope Group, which has $500 million in sales and ranks among China's largest and most prominent private business groups. After WTO entry, Liu says, "resources should be allocated according to the market and many rules and regulations will have to be changed". One can only hope that his optimism proves justified.

China needs financial-sector reform in order to make this transition. Its banking system is extremely weak, with bad loans accounting for at least 25–40% of total lending (and about the same percentage of GDP). A series of scandals and other problems in the late 1990s revealed systemic weaknesses in this structure. China is already trying to improve its domestic banks. It has hived off bad loans into special-purpose vehicles (asset-management companies) tasked with disposing of these assets. Beijing plans overseas stock-market listings for parts of the banks in the hope that more transparency and the scrutiny of outside investors will mean better performance. If these reform plans are carried to their logical conclusion, it would mean a financial system that made credit decisions based on strict commercial principles rather than on the basis of political imperatives or personal connections. WTO membership alone won't bring this about — the world is full of financial institutions that make lending decisions for political or personal reasons — but it will push China further in this direction. Financial-sector reform is hard, as Japan's decade-long difficulties show. Cleaning up a troubled financial system means putting many people out of work. Not doing it right is a recipe for failure in overall economic reform. It requires reform of the legal system, instituting such things as bankruptcy procedures, minority shareholder rights, insider-trading laws and other aspects of corporate governance. Up till now, China has been able to get by without an efficient system to allocate capital because of large inflows of foreign direct investment, capital which *is* allocated efficiently. But with or without WTO status, there are serious limits to growth if the financial and legal systems aren't fixed.

ঽ৶   ঽ৶   ঽ৶

Acceptance by the WTO won't mean an overnight transformation of China. Skeptics have valid reasons for worrying about China's capacity to implement the agreement. For example, despite a landmark and hard-fought intellectual-property rights agreement between the US and China in 1995, intellectual-property piracy remains a major problem.[10] The legal and administrative challenges that China faces are similar to those that took decades, or even centuries, to work out in the advanced economies of the West. And the scale of the problems is enormous. The 85 million workers in state-owned enterprises alone outnumber the entire populations of most nations. The 900 million rural dwellers constitute a number that is more than three times larger than any other nation on earth except India. China's problems are enormous, but the skill with which it has navigated its way through the first two decades of reforms provides some reason to believe that progress can continue. Of course, past performance is no guarantee of future success. For now, with the coming of the WTO, China moves into deeper, faster-moving waters.

---

[1] Claude Smadja, an advisor to the World Economic Forum, suggested the analogy to the 1964 weapons test at an Asia Society meeting in Hong Kong on June 18, 2001.

   Throughout this book, we have provided citations except in those instances where information is broadly accepted and available. We have not cited information that comes from personal meetings and interviews, though we have endeavored wherever possible to make it clear from the context that these are the sources. In some cases, however, certain sensitivities made this impossible.

   This chapter draws on a broad variety of sources. The following works were particularly useful: John King Fairbank, *China: A New History*, Cambridge, Massachusetts, Harvard University Press, 1992; Graham Hutchings, *Modern China: A Companion to a Rising Power*, London, Penguin

Books, 2000; Stanley B. Lubman, *Bird in a Cage: Legal Reform in China After Mao*, Stanford, California, Stanford University Press, 1999; World Bank, *China 2020* (seven volumes), Washington, D.C., The World Bank, 1997.

² "China's Prospective WTO Accession", in *World Economic Outlook*, Washington, D.C., International Monetary Fund, 2000, pp. 27–28. For a discussion of the higher estimates, see Chapter 4. Also, although textile export restrictions should be eliminated on December 31, 2004, the United States negotiated a series of restrictions on Chinese textile and clothing exports until the end of 2008. See Chapter 5.

³ See, for example, Gordon G. Chang, *The Coming Collapse of China*, New York, N.Y., Random House, 2001.

⁴ This data is from Angus Maddison, *Monitoring the World Economy*, Paris, Organization for Economic Cooperation and Development, 1995, p. 30.

⁵ Quoted in Jonathan Spence, *The Search for Modern China*, New York, N.Y., W.W. Norton, 1990, p. 122.

⁶ The "treated unjustly" phrase comes from Hu Yaobang, as quoted in Hutchings, *op.cit.*, p. 93.

⁷ The World Bank, *China 2020: Development Challenges In The New Century*, Washington, D.C., The World Bank, 1997, p. ix.

⁸ *Ibid.*, p. 71.

⁹ The World Bank, *China 2020: China Engaged*, Washington, D.C., The World Bank, 1997. p. 36, estimates that China would forgo gains of US$1.2 trillion by 2020 if it integrates more slowly.

¹⁰ A great deal has been written on China's problems with intellectual-property rights. For a recent look at large-scale counterfeiting, see Dexter Roberts et al., "China's Pirates", *BusinessWeek*, June 5, 2000.

CHAPTER 2

The WTO:
Promise and Peril

I n the alphabet soup of acronyms that makes up the
world of international organizations, the WTO at first
glance presents a pretty unlikely target. The
organization only came into being in 1995 and has a staff
of just over 500, who work on the shores of Switzerland's
Lake Geneva. Yet to hear protestors tell it, the WTO is a
powerful cabal that's a front for rich nations and large
corporations, one that is helping to drive down global
wages, strip countries of their autonomy and destroy the
environment. Opponents vilify the WTO, along with the
World Bank and the IMF, as the enforcer of a cruel new
world order. They claim that the WTO is intent on running
roughshod over the interests of everyone from French
cheese makers to democracy activists in China.

In fact, the WTO is the torchbearer for one of the
most remarkable achievements in the 20th century — the
establishment of a relatively free international trade order
that is governed by clear rules and doesn't allow for
favoritism or discrimination. Although it's still a young
organization, the WTO reflects the vision set out six decades
ago by US President Franklin Delano Roosevelt and British
Prime Minister Winston Churchill in their Atlantic Charter

of August 1941. Having seen how the promise of globalization had soured in the run-up to World War I and the way in which protectionism had exacerbated political tensions and set the stage for World War II, the two Western leaders promised "to endeavor the enjoyment by all States, great or small, victor or vanquished, of access, on equal terms, to the trade and to the raw materials of the world, which are needed for their economic prosperity". The two men also vowed "to bring about the fullest collaboration between all nations in the economic field with the object of securing, for all, improved labor standards, economic advancement and social security".

Beneath the dry language are some remarkable concepts. The idea of free trade and the notion that big nations shouldn't be able to discriminate against smaller ones marked a momentous shift in thinking. Churchill and Roosevelt's Atlantic Charter appeared barely a decade after Herbert Hoover had signed, on June 16, 1930, the disastrous Smoot-Hawley tariff bill. Hoover had backed the bill, saying the US "cannot successfully compete against foreign producers because of lower foreign wages and a lower cost of production". The result was an unmitigated disaster. Other countries responded with retaliatory tariff hikes. Trade fell 70% between 1930 and 1933, fueling a global depression. By the end of the decade the first shots had been fired in what soon became World War II, the deadliest and most widespread conflict the world had ever seen.

With peace in 1945 came a chance to build new international institutions. The United Nations and the World Bank emerged out of the post-war rubble. Unfortunately, a strong world trade body remained stillborn. But free-trade proponents pushed on under the auspices of the

General Agreement on Tariffs and Trade (GATT), which was founded in 1947 but had no power to enforce its rules and thus was a disappointment to advocates of freer trade. Since then, GATT and its successor, the WTO, have buttressed more than a half-century of unparalleled global growth and prosperity. Trade saves lives. Freer trade is a principal reason that 700 million people were lifted out of poverty between 1990 and 1998. There's little doubt that freer trade spurs economic growth, given conducive existing conditions; the most that critics can say is that fervent advocates of free trade sometimes overstate its benefits, and that those benefits are inequitably shared. But no one can credibly argue that trade in goods should be more limited.[1]

The free-trade boom that Roosevelt, Churchill and other committed internationalists set off underpinned one of the most prosperous half-centuries in human history. Global per capita income has nearly tripled in the past 50 years, even as population has exploded. Life expectancy has increased by 20 years and infant mortality has fallen by two-thirds. At the same time, the value of world trade has surged 15 times and global economic output has multiplied six times. The burden of proof should be on those who want to restrict trade, not those who would liberalize it.

Free trade is one of the most effective ways to accelerate economic development. But those people who work on trade liberalization need to take heed of the global backlash. The best way to do that is to ensure that developing countries truly get a fair deal with trade. Ensuring that the benefits of trade flow to those who need it the most isn't only good economic sense, but also makes good political sense. It's essential to ensure that trade produces benefits to those at the bottom of the economic ladder if the momentum for more open trade is to continue.

The need to spur trade, and thus growth, is pressing: about 700 million people from the developing world will enter the workforce — or at least try to enter the workforce — in the next decade. That's larger than the total developed-world workforce today. Only a more open global economy will provide the growth needed to ensure that these people find jobs. While the WTO's critics would have us believe that the organization acts primarily to advance multi-national interests, the WTO ideally should be a neutral body that represents the interests of small countries and great powers alike. Developing countries gave up a good deal of ground in the Uruguay Round (UR), the trade negotiations that began in 1987 and resulted in the establishment of the WTO. It's clear that the next major task of the WTO is to ensure that the next trade round benefits the poorer nations as much as possible.

THE WTO AND ITS DISCONTENTS

Trade negotiations are arcane and tedious, typically attracting little more than a passing mention even in the business and financial press. All that changed on a tumultuous late-November day in Seattle in 1999, when fierce street demonstrations thrust the WTO into the limelight. The demonstrations highlighted the deep suspicion held by many people around the world toward free trade and the seemingly unstoppable march toward globalization.

The protests broke out when trade ministers and senior officials representing more than 130 countries gathered to try to launch a new round of trade talks aimed at further liberalization. Thousands of protestors were determined to stop the new round of negotiations. The protestors comprised a diverse, multi-national group, ranging from Tibetan monks to small business people to elderly Gray Panthers, labor groups and environmentalists. Thanks to a smattering of violent protestors, what likely would have been a sedate meeting became a scene of broken shop windows and trade delegates imprisoned in their hotel rooms. Suddenly the mutterings of labor unions, environmental organizations and an assortment of anti-capitalists became world news. The "Battle in Seattle" changed the politics of world trade for the foreseeable future.

The push for a new round of trade talks was faltering and probably wouldn't have gotten off the ground in any event because of deep disagreements among the major participants. The Ministerial Statement was full of unsettled areas — there were more than 100 of what negotiators refer to as "bracketed areas". The brackets are left blank to mark areas of disagreement during international trade negotiations, and are filled in only when agreement is reached. Usually it would take a few weeks to iron out 100 brackets, not the four days that the delegates had in Seattle. Add to that President Bill Clinton's statement, made just as the meeting was about to kick off, that the US would insist on making labor rights part of any new agreement, with trade sanctions for violators, and hopes for the launch of a new trade round in Seattle were doomed before the meeting began. The new round was dashed not because of the protestors outside but mainly because of the vast disagreements inside the meeting room.

But the street battles were what grabbed the world's

attention. The US delegation couldn't even make it to the conference center for the scheduled opening, forcing the postponement of the opening ceremony. Any remaining hopes for a launch of the so-called Millennium Round were shattered. And in the mythology of the anti-globalization movement, the protestors had stopped a new round of talks from beginning. More important, the protests crystallized the general unease throughout much of the world with the pace of globalization. Not since the anti-war, anti-establishment battles of the 1960s and 1970s had policy makers in the US and Europe faced popular discontent of this sort. And never had there been a protest movement that drew on these sorts of global roots. Lori Wallach, one of the protest organizers, claimed that the anti-WTO coalition represented groups from 25 countries.[2]

Emboldened, protestors have pressed on. Every big trade and globalization meeting now features its set-piece protests. The list of cities that have become battlegrounds reads like a globetrotter's itinerary. After Seattle, protestors next disrupted the World Bank/IMF meeting in Prague and the World Economic Forum in Melbourne, which both took place the following September. Protestors besieged the picturesque Swiss ski town of Davos at the annual gathering of the global great and good at the World Economic Forum in early 2001. Next came Quebec, where an April summit designed to promote free trade in the Americas featured the increasingly familiar riot police and coils of barbed wire separating the global elite from those who would destroy their vision of a borderless world. The Swedish city of Gothenburg endured even worse violence when European Union (EU) leaders met in June 2001 to discuss further European integration. And at the G-8 leaders' summit in Genoa in July that year, a protestor was killed amidst ferocious clashes.

"The 1990s began in Berlin and ended in Seattle," writes *Foreign Policy* editor Moises Naim. "In Berlin, a crowd tore down a wall built to contain democracy and free markets. In Seattle, another crowd rioted against the World Trade Organization in an effort to rebuild walls that might shield them from the ills unleashed by 'globalization' ... Thus, a decade that began with great hopes about the global spread of capitalism ended with widespread apprehension about it. What happened?"[3]

What happened is that the benefits of free trade are slow in coming and unequally distributed, while the costs are quick and sharp. Overall, inequality is narrowing, not widening.[4] Yet during the past two decades, while the rich got quite a bit richer, many poorer countries stagnated. The United Nations Human Development Report calculates that from 1980 to 1996, only 33 countries sustained 3% compound growth. Meanwhile, 59 countries (mostly in sub-Saharan Africa, Eastern Europe and the Commonwealth of Independent States) saw GNP per capita actually fall. "Economic integration is thus dividing developing and transition economies into those that are benefiting from global opportunities and those that are not," concludes the United Nations report.[5]

Meanwhile, the pace of change has accelerated. The pains of economic dislocation are easier to see and are more keenly felt. Anti-trade protests reflect public unease with free trade and globalization. But the demonstrations also amplify this discomfort, this sense that change is accelerating and that the world is spinning out of control. There's a belief that, as globalization skeptic Martin Khor puts it, "environmental, social and cultural problems have been made worse by the workings of the global free-market economy". The unstated view among many people, and not just those out there on the streets, is that we would do better by returning to a simpler time. That nostalgia is fueled by the sense that there is a widening gap in wealth and income within both developed and developing countries. It's understandable why many people want to slow the pace of change, or even stop it altogether.[6]

Yet inward-looking policies are no answer. Trade and openness don't in and of themselves guarantee growth. But without them, growth will be slower. There is a strong correlation between openness and growth. To take one of many examples, a study of 18 developing economies with open regimes showed high levels of growth in the 1980s and 1990s. Other developing countries in the study grew slowly in the 1980s and declined in the 1990s.[7]

FREER TRADE ON A GLOBAL SCALE

Trade is the most obvious evidence of globalization. The costs of free trade are dramatic and visible. It's easy to see jobs flee from rich countries only to re-appear in a lower-wage site. The United States has lost much of its steel industry to increased competition from countries like Japan, South Korea and Brazil. The US shoe industry is a shell of its former self. Meanwhile, steel mills in South Korea run at full blast and subcontractors at Nike alone employ hundreds of thousands of people around the world. Transnational companies, ones whose operations cross borders, now account for a full one-third of world output and two-thirds of world trade.[8]

While the costs of trade are concentrated and painfully apparent, the benefits to consumers are diffused. Whether it's cheaper, better steel for computer cases and refrigerators, better choice in sporting shoes or better cars, it's hard to argue that more competition is a bad thing. As Ambassador Charlene Barshefsky, former US Trade Representative (USTR), put it: "Exports let us serve larger markets and are generally associated with higher-paying jobs; imports increase competition and economic efficiency, dampen inflation, and raise the standard of living, especially for the poorest families."[9] And the long-term record of the US economy shows that openness to foreign trade has paid dramatic benefits. It's difficult to separate the impact of trade alone. But the economic growth record of the more open American economy over the past 20 years compares favorably with the other two major economic blocs, Japan and Europe. This isn't just a pro-business agenda, as anti-globalization advocates claim. It's an agenda that benefits countries as a whole.

The so-called Washington Consensus of the 1980s and 1990s believed that more liberalization alone was better. Liberalization would lead to more economic growth and a better life for all. But this focus on tearing down barriers ignored the lesson that development and growth also require hard political choices. And they require institutional building blocks, such as clean, efficient government and a good legal system. The task of globalization advocates now is to see that the foundations for growth are put in place. The WTO can help in this process, but it's only one block in a large building effort.

The WTO also limits the likelihood of a cycle of vicious retaliation like the one that worsened the Depression of the 1930s. "In the Asian financial crisis of 1997–99, with

40% of the world in recession, the respect WTO members had for their commitments kept open the markets necessary for affected nations to recover," notes Barshefsky. "Thus the system of mutual benefit and rule of law represented by the WTO helped prevent a cycle of protection and retaliation like that of the 1930s; and ultimately to avert the political strife that can erupt in economic crisis."

The high visibility of multinational corporations around the globe and their role in promoting and engaging in free trade makes them obvious targets for those who challenge the benefits of freer trade. Better communications, especially e-mail and the Internet, make it far easier to publicize abuses. Activists find it easier to mobilize support in the West against a multinational, such as Nike, than against a little-known domestic company in, say, Indonesia. The fact that the conditions in a Nike factory aren't perfect, and that abuses do take place — in vivid contrast to the image that a marketing-driven company is trying to portray — makes it that much easier to mobilize protestors. The reluctance of many companies to take more responsibility for conditions in their factories (and their subcontractors' factories) only adds to protestors' suspicions. But this isn't an argument against more liberal trade. It's an argument in favor of improved working conditions in developing countries and a reminder that multinational corporations don't have a monopoly on the fruits of globalization.

Freer trade and the high-profile visibility of a WTO that has the power to act as an international trade court also provoke fears that national sovereignty is being eroded by a supra-national rule-making body. The dispute between the European Union and the United States over genetically modified agricultural products cuts to the heart of the debate over whether international or domestic (or, in this case, regional) standards should prevail. Critics in rich countries fear that the WTO will prohibit them from adopting their own environmental standards. US legislation to prohibit the imports of fish caught by methods that kill dolphins, sea turtles and shrimp, which penalized Thailand and Malaysia, has already been struck down as an improper trade barrier because the WTO prohibits trade practices that discriminate against a product based on the method used to produce it. But the issue of trade and the environment promises to remain an important one. On the other side, developing nations fear that this new international order will reflect the concerns of the rich world and rob them of their ability to adopt appropriate policies for national development.

The WTO is an easy target. Its job is to be trade's global cop. Because it has the power to impose binding decisions that it can back up with trade sanctions, the WTO has far more power that its predecessor (GATT) to see that trade violators are punished. But it's a young and relatively weak organization that relies for its strength on the willingness of its more than 140 members to play by the rules. Protestors attack the WTO for issues, such as labor, that do not and should not lie within the purview of the trade body out of the misguided belief that the WTO is more powerful than it is.

The WTO's critics are particularly suspicious of intellectual-property rights accords, which for now appear to primarily benefit multinationals from rich countries, at the expense of people's lives in developing countries. The controversy over patent protection for pharmaceuticals is an understandably contentious issue. Under the new intellectual-property rights accord agreed to in the Uruguay Round — known as TRIPs (Trade-Related Aspects of Intellectual Property Rights Agreement) — restrictions on drug manufacturing have been tightened considerably. Pharmaceutical companies say that they cannot afford to develop new drugs without the certainty that generic knock-off producers won't then rob them of their discovery. But it's morally indefensible to deny drugs to treat life-threatening diseases in poor countries. TRIPs could be made more useful if provisions in the agreement were fully implemented so that both the protection of rights *and* the accessibility to intellectual property were guaranteed. We should expect to see more conflict in this area.

We must ensure that legitimate concerns are met, whether it's inside or outside of the WTO. These include issues such as the environment and labor, which don't belong within the purview of a WTO that already has more on its agenda than it can properly handle. These concerns also include ensuring that trade truly benefits poor and developing countries, which is a proper matter for the WTO. Besides ensuring that freer trade benefits more people, advocates of a liberal trading order also need to do a better job of explaining those benefits to the public. Governments and corporations are on the defensive. Corporations, too, are often reluctant to talk about their foreign operations for fear that this will inflame labor tensions at home. Governments are more concerned with defusing protests than developing a free-trade agenda.

The militant, sometimes violent, street protestors are not really what the world needs to worry about. These protestors are small in number and don't have significant popular support. What we need to worry about is a broader backlash against globalization, one that would prevent the further development of free trade and the economic development it brings.

Legitimate though many of the protestors' critiques are, the answer isn't to freeze change or hark back to a mythical golden past. First, we need to articulate more clearly the concrete benefits of freer trade and ensure that those benefits are shared as widely as possible. Policy makers also need to ensure that the WTO is a fair deal for all, not just a club where the wealthy nations essentially make the rules and impose them on others.

Freer trade has helped end poverty. The Evian Group, a coalition of free-trade advocates, notes that the general market opening across the world between 1990 and 1998 has helped to ensure that 700 million people have been lifted out of poverty. So, too, has more cross-border investment. Foreign direct investment has exploded from $58 billion in 1982 — only a little more than China alone now receives annually — to $865 billion in 1999. The problem is that freer trade hasn't delivered on its promise for the poor world, in large part because of continuing protectionism in the rich world, especially its farmers and its textile and clothing industries. Another reason is the lack of domestic policies in the developing world that build links between trade and the domestic economy, especially by ensuring that investment and trade create jobs. But it's the rich world, which has been a major beneficiary of freer trade, that is complaining most loudly. The irony is that, traditionally, labor and environmentalists have been internationalists. But rather than embracing free trade as a way of pursuing the development agenda, they often seem to be pursuing an agenda that will ultimately work against free trade.[10]

The suspicion that activists in the West are, above all, protectionists has set up a potentially dangerous dynamic where developing countries now question the West's sincerity in using trade to advance development. Malaysia has been one of the most obvious beneficiaries of free trade. Since 1980, it has transformed itself from an economy built on tin mines and palm-oil plantations into a leading electronics exporter. It has embraced free trade, in most areas, and has welcomed foreign investment. Per capita incomes have shot up and the country in many respects stands as a model for what sound macroeconomic policies and free trade can accomplish.

Yet as the economy was rocked by the Asian financial crisis, and Western activists and politicians began to agitate for protecting labor rights in exchange for free trade, the country's long-serving prime minister, Mahathir Mohamad, increasingly began to question the benefits of free trade and globalization: "This new religion demands complete and unquestioning obedience from the poor and the weak, especially when they need money ... There is so much globalization nonsense. There are so many corporate giants hiding their teeth and intent on gobbling us up ... The second great Asian colonialism is upon us." Mahathir proclaimed that since the advent of the Asian crisis, "today there are no more economic tigers in Asia" because "they have been destroyed" by the West.[11]

❧   ❧   ❧

It wasn't supposed to be like this. When Churchill and Roosevelt laid out their grand vision for a free international trade order six decades ago, the idea was to use trade as a force for peace and prosperity. Originally, the International Trade Organization (ITO) was supposed to be set up immediately after World War II, at the same time as the International Bank for Reconstruction and Development (now known as the World Bank) and the IMF. But the US pulled out because of Congressional objections to surrendering its authority over trade policy to an international body. Instead of a strong ITO, delegates agreed to set up the General Agreement on Tariffs and Trade, which was a voluntary club rather than a legally binding organization and thus had no teeth to enforce its decisions. Despite its limitations, GATT played an extremely important role in reducing industrial tariffs, particularly among richer countries.

But developing countries' interests played only a minor role in GATT negotiations. For many years, textiles and clothing, which account for a substantial part of developing countries' total exports, were kept out of the normal GATT system because of a restrictive quota-driven system, known as the Multi-Fiber Arrangement (MFA), that the US and Europe initiated to protect their domestic industries. Agriculture, a critical export for many developing nations, wasn't even taken up in the negotiations until the Uruguay Round was launched in 1987. Then, in exchange for negotiations designed to liberalize trade in agriculture and textiles, developing countries agreed to developed countries' requests that intellectual-property rights and investment measures be put on the bargaining table.

By the end of the Uruguay Round, the rich world had

given little ground on agriculture, even though the US and the European Union account for roughly 80% of all agricultural subsidies, which total a staggering $360 billion annually in the rich world. But developing countries accepted the new agreements on intellectual-property rights (TRIPs) and investment (Trade-Related Investment Measures, or TRIMs). These require significant adjustments in developing countries' policies, with little obvious pay-off for these countries. In general, developing countries contend, not surprisingly, that benefits from trade rounds haven't been equally distributed.

Perhaps the most important outcome of the Uruguay Round was the decision to set up the World Trade Organization, which came into effect from January 1, 1995. The WTO represented a big advance from GATT. First, all of its agreements are binding. Under GATT, which had no such power, some members didn't even sign up to obligations that were agreed in trade rounds. By contrast, WTO members are required to adopt all commitments that the body negotiates.

Second, under WTO there can be a continuation of successive trade negotiations in areas that are under discussion, rather than waiting for the launch of a new trade round. A new round sets out new negotiating parameters and can involve new areas for negotiation. Recently, there have been successful sectoral negotiations for financial and telecommunications services, despite a failure to agree on the launch of a new trade round. The so-called built-in agenda left over from the Uruguay Round in agriculture and services has, since the year 2000, been picked up by WTO negotiators. This has meant more continuity in trade negotiations and could mean more rapid liberalization.

Third, the newly adopted Dispute Settlement Body helps to resolve disagreements. If no resolution can be reached and a member is found to violate WTO rules, the organization has the power to authorize the complaining country to take retaliatory trade sanctions. First, the Dispute Settlement Body encourages and allows members to negotiate a solution. If that fails, a dispute-settlement panel adjudicates disputes, referring to an appellate body for a final ruling. All of these final rulings must be adopted by the parties involved. The establishment of this international trade court should be celebrated, not loathed. Its aim is to bring rules into the world of trade, a world where the weak previously had no recourse against the strong.

A NEW DEAL FOR TRADE

One of the problems of the trade debate today is that too often it is only about trade. When trade negotiators and developed-country officials discuss the benefits of free trade, or the reasons for a new round of world trade negotiations, they mostly emphasize the fact that trade liberalization leads to more trade. Unfortunately, this doesn't say very much about how much it improves the lives of human beings. We shouldn't just say, for instance, that trade liberalization will lead to more trade in steel, clothing or shoes. We need to know that increased trade will lead to more investment and a more balanced international division of labor, allowing countries to specialize in areas in which they have comparative advantages. We should ask whether increased trade has improved skill levels and social welfare, or contributed toward the creation of jobs and, thus, incomes. In other words, does trade help the process of sustainable development?

If trade cannot help solve economic and social problems, if it doesn't lead to more income, more investment and more jobs, especially in poorer countries, then it's hard to imagine that there will be support for further trade liberalization. After all, most countries are faced with plenty of other pressing economic and political priorities. Selling a skeptical population on trade agreements, which are by nature disruptive, isn't easy for any country. Since the 1994 completion of the Uruguay Round, which established the WTO, conditions in low-income countries haven't improved in a way that would make them particularly enthusiastic about further liberalization. In fact, as noted above, in more than 50 of the poorest countries economic conditions have deteriorated. Public and private debt has been rising and prices of the world's major commodities have been falling. Export subsidies for farm products have been rising in the more advanced economies, leading to a drop in the prices of commodities sold by the developing nations. Official development aid has also declined.

Although foreign direct investment has risen, most of it has gone to only a small number of countries. The United Nations Development Program (UNDP) calculates that more than 80% of the foreign direct investment in developing and transition economies (a group that includes Eastern Europe and the former Soviet Union) went to just 20% of the countries, with China getting far more than any other. And, contrary to what some of the more unsubtle proponents of free trade imply, simply trading more doesn't automatically lead to development. Some of those countries that have been left behind are deeply integrated into the world trading system. Sub-Saharan Africa has a higher trade-to-GDP measure (29% in the 1990s) than Latin America

(15%). But the UNDP notes that because Africa's exports are mostly commodities, and most foreign investment is in mining, "the region's apparent integration is actually a vulnerability to the whims of the primary commodity markets".[12]

Meanwhile, health conditions have deteriorated sharply in many countries, particularly in Africa, where more than 20 million people are infected with HIV/AIDS. Also in Africa, there are still pockets of tuberculosis and malaria. Apart from its terrible human cost, the deteriorating health situation has also damaged economic productivity. Structural unemployment remains pervasive, with jobless rates reaching 30–40% in many African countries. Even in South Africa, one of the continent's most advanced economies, unemployment among black men was 29% in 1995.[13]

Trade can play a role in solving these problems by, for instance, promoting productive foreign direct investment. But unless we can establish clear-cut linkages between increased trade and higher levels of employment, it will be very difficult for those who want freer trade to make a convincing case for it. It won't be enough to demonstrate that trade leads to greater economic efficiency. One can also create efficiency by introducing new technology. But while new technology often increases productivity, it doesn't always increase employment and balanced, sustainable development. Besides creating jobs, trade should facilitate dynamic changes in developing economies, such as promoting a wider range of higher-quality tradable products.

Rich countries need to lower barriers to trade, especially to goods such as clothes and agricultural products that the poorest countries can produce most efficiently. The World Bank recently compiled a depressing list of some of the high-tariff products in the rich countries. The list includes major farm products, such as meat, sugar, dairy products and chocolate, products which commonly have 100%-plus tariffs in the rich countries. Fruits and vegetables also typically attract stiff tariffs, all the way up to 180% for bananas going to the European Union. Peanuts face tariffs of 550% in Japan and 132% in the United States. Textiles, clothing and footwear not only have tariff rates in the 15–30% range for a large number of products, but, even worse, they also must contend with quotas that restrict their exports. Tariffs are bad, because they raise the cost of trade. But quotas are worse because they place an artificial limit on how much of a product can be traded — even if a consumer wants to pay a higher price, quota restrictions can prohibit imports. It's certainly no coincidence that these quotas are in areas where developing countries have a comparative advantage.

Having preached the virtues of free trade, it's up to the rich countries to allow the developing world to practice it. The staggering $360 billion that the rich countries of the world spend each year protecting domestic agriculture dwarfs the amount they devote to foreign aid. "Many of the world's poorest countries have failed to win the benefits of increased openness to the global economy, due to their own policy and institutional shortcomings, but also importantly, the severe impact of protectionist barriers against their goods in industrial countries," notes Uri Dadush, Director of the World Bank's Economic Policy and Prospects Group. "These trade barriers act as a major roadblock for developing countries wanting to get greater quantities of their textiles and agricultural goods into the lucrative import markets of industrial countries."[14]

The problem isn't too much globalization; it's too little. The least-developed countries account for less than 0.5% of the world's exports and they receive less than 1% of the world's total foreign direct investment. "The main losers in today's very unequal world are not those who have been exposed too much to globalization," says UN Secretary-General Kofi Annan. "They are those who have been left out." And while for a long time many critics of trade liberalization contended that developing countries would be forever stuck selling raw materials, the reality is that 75% of total exports from developing countries are manufactured goods. These are, for the most part, labor-intensive industries, where wage levels are often low and the potential for abuse is high. But the experience of East Asia over the last 40 years shows that it's possible to use an export-oriented manufacturing base as a platform to develop an increasingly sophisticated and prosperous economy. Indeed, as the developed world increasingly trades in services, developing countries like China and its East Asian neighbors are becoming the workshop of the world.

THE WTO AND LABOR RIGHTS

One of the most controversial issues is tying labor rights to the WTO. Trade is supposed to improve living standards. So, the WTO's critics say, it's only fair that the WTO back up the promise of better living conditions with concrete action. Their equation is simple: no labor rights, no free trade.

Developing countries don't see it that way. They see thinly disguised protectionism. They're afraid that the labor-rights standard will be used to keep their goods out of rich markets. In fact, injecting more politics into trade would almost certainly ensure that the strong, developed countries get their way. Only stronger countries can afford to politicize these issues. It's easier for them to take their domestic interests and bring pressure to bear on international organizations.

It's instructive to look at the result when the US tied increases in Cambodia's quotas for garment exports to improved labor standards. The results have been mixed. Labor standards, conditions and wages are better than they would be otherwise. But, understandably in a country where the monthly minimum wage is just $45, they haven't improved enough to satisfy US labor unions and human-rights activists. The quota increase, not surprisingly, became more politicized than it would otherwise have been. The experience has left neither activists nor developing countries happy. It's also important to note that the US was using textile quotas to try to ensure better behavior. Given that these are slated to expire at the end of 2004, this strategy certainly isn't a long-term solution to the issue.

More broadly, some critics in the West even want to use the WTO as a club to force countries to live up to international standards in a variety of areas. Lori Wallach claims that the strategy of economic engagement with China "has been a total bust". While the US administration told the public that more trade with China would open up the society, Wallach claims it hasn't happened. "During this period when the free market would allegedly enhance their freedoms, we've seen the opposite." She calls for trade regulations that would mark some "basic rules of the road about prison labor, about basic human rights, political right to organize, freedom of religious expression, freedom of communications, access to information — the things that you really need to make a capitalistic society work in the long term".

Wallach thinks that there is a lot of "bad trade". Some of her examples are cogent, as when she spotlights hidden subsidies that she says encourage environmentally damaging trade. But some of them are far-fetched, at best. Her classic example of bad trade in China is "when a company can make an arrangement with the Chinese government to have at a People's Liberation Army work camp a bunch of Tiananmen Square college kids who are incredibly smart, and literally under the gun, making blue jeans or toys, at no expense to the company, except whatever it costs for the contract with the People's Liberation Army. The profits are enormous." Wallach would use the WTO's Article 20, which provides for legitimate exemption from trade rules, to slap an embargo on goods made in conditions of forced labor. "I wouldn't use tariffs. I would just say: Until these conditions change, these goods are not sellable here." In fact, WTO regulations already allow countries to prohibit the import of goods made by prison labor and, during the 1990s, the US did prohibit the import of some Chinese goods that it found were produced by prison labor. Article 20, however, is supposed to be used for issues such as natural disasters and national security. Many non-governmental organizations (NGOs) think Article 20 isn't broad enough and would like to be able to use it for trade-related environmental problems.

Even while acknowledging the complexity of the issue, there is little evidence to support the contention that China has seen freedoms diminished in the past decade, a fact that seriously undercuts Wallach's argument. The reality of most China trade is far from the caricature Wallach paints. For the most part, workers in the export manufacturing sector are young women who would count themselves fortunate if they had a high-school education. Most are from poor farming villages and have willingly emigrated to one of the coastal factories. They work long hours, under conditions that range from difficult to appalling, but enough of them manage to save a fair amount of money during the several years that they work in the factories that the jobs are highly sought after. Certainly, there are abuses, and they should be exposed and rectified. Increasingly, both the Chinese and foreign media do just that. But to ignore the role that trade has played in lifting hundreds of millions of Chinese out of poverty, and of giving young women in particular more financial independence and thus freedom, is to mock the promise that free trade holds.[15] No, China isn't democratic. Yes, there are ways in which foreign pressure can push China in a more liberal direction. But the WTO isn't one of them. To overtly politicize the WTO would be to muddy its mission and risk seriously damaging the organization. There already are enough international organizations that accomplish very little.

Wallach wants to use the sledgehammer of the annual US Congressional review of China's trading status to force change. The annual review of what was known as Most Favored Nation (MFN) status, and is now known as Normal Trading Relations (NTR), will be eliminated once China enters the WTO, because it's incompatible with the organization's fundamental principle that no member nation can be discriminated against. But more broadly, Wallach's sentiments betray a seductive and dangerous illusion that the world trade body can solve all of society's ills. If general and largely insurmountable hurdles are set up for developing countries to jump, the promise of free trade will remain stillborn.[16]

In fact, China already has signed a number of binding international agreements that should ensure compliance with a broad range of human rights of the sort that Wallach would like to see. The issue is whether its trading rights should be suspended to try to force compliance on these other issues. At heart, it's a philosophical debate. We believe that the benefits of free trade are so powerful, and the difficulties in maintaining and extending a liberal trade regime so difficult, that loading the trade agenda with this additional baggage is counterproductive. After all, the WTO is in the business of promoting trade, not of finding reasons to decrease trade.

In recent years, there has been a great deal of research that demonstrates the complexity of the issue of labor rights and trade. The studies don't support the view that developing countries can improve their trade performance by violating basic labor rights in a bid to reduce their labor costs and make their exports more competitive. On the contrary, it has been found that those countries that don't embrace, or haven't fully adopted, core labor standards cannot attract new investment, cannot enhance their productive capacities, and will mostly fail to advance or improve their trade performance.[17]

Countries that adopt core labor standards, such as the right to collective bargaining, abolition of child labor and the freedom of assembly, have registered strong improvements in their trade performance in the last few years. These findings suggest that there shouldn't be a direct linkage in trade agreements between trade and labor standards, a position that was endorsed at the WTO's first ministerial conference in Singapore in 1996. At that meeting, WTO members reiterated their commitment to core labor standards, but said that the issue should be handled by the International Labor Organization (ILO). In the meantime, the ILO is being strengthened so that it can deal with labor violations more forcefully. Investigation teams are being sent into countries where there are official complaints of labor-rights violations. More can and should be done. But there is no place in a trade-promoting body for what will inevitably be highly politicized, and often subjective, judgments about an area that is outside both the WTO's jurisdiction and the technical competence of its staff.

From the point of view of developing countries, there are many practical reasons why it makes no sense to link trade and labor standards, besides the obvious danger that developed countries would politicize the process. In many developing countries, the unofficial labor market is very much larger than the official labor market, but the authorities only monitor conditions in the official market. If trading partners apply sanctions to countries that violate core labor rights, they won't necessarily solve the problem, because the violations may simply migrate into the unofficial market. Factories that exploit child labor, for instance, could simply go deeper underground. Also, there is evidence that basic labor violations are less severe in the tradable sector (anything that can be traded across borders) than in the non-tradable sector (purely domestic goods and services).

A more effective approach may be to reward countries that enforce labor rights, rather than penalize those that don't. These countries could be given trade preferences and assistance, so that manufacturers would have an incentive to improve their labor standards still further. For example, the European Union's system of preferences reduces tariffs by at least 10 percentage points (and for some products even more sharply) for qualified developing countries. Labor standards are one of the factors evaluated in deciding whether to extend the favorable treatment.

One of the best ways to tackle the problem of child labor is to increase periods of compulsory education. Thailand, for instance, is expanding compulsory education to 12 years, from six years not too long ago. Effectively, this eradicates child labor because the children are obliged to go to school. Although many poor parents feel that they cannot afford to let their children attend school, because the family needs even the pitiful income that the child can provide, education is one of the best investments that a family or a society can make. Domestic policies mandating education can further that goal.

---

[1] For a review of the data, see The World Bank, *Global Economic Prospects and the Developing Countries 2001*, Washington, D.C., The World Bank, 2001, Box 2.1, p. 52. The 700 million figure comes from the Evian Group's *Evian VI Plenary Meeting*, Montreux, Switzerland, April 20–22, 2001, p. 2 (mimeo).

[2] All the Lori Wallach remarks in this chapter are from "Lori's War", a lengthy interview that appeared in *Foreign Policy*, Spring 2000.

[3] *Ibid.*, Editor's Note.

[4] *Eliminating World Poverty: Making Globalisation Work for the Poor, A White Paper on International Development, Presented to Parliament by the Secretary of State for International Development*, The Stationery Office, London, 2000, p. 17.

5   United Nations Development Program, *Human Development Report 1999*, New York, N.Y., Oxford University Press, 1999, p. 31.

6   Martin Khor, *Globalization and the South: Some Critical Issues*, Penang, Malaysia, Third World Network, 2000, p. i.

7   Cited in *Eliminating World Poverty, op.cit.*, p. 66.

8   *Ibid.*, p. 15.

9   "Director's Forum Lecture on Trade and Development", Ambassador Charlene Barshefsky, US Trade Representative, The Peace Corps, Washington, D.C., June 20, 2000.

10   The figures are from *Evian VI Plenary Meeting, op.cit.*, p. 2.

11   Mahathir's remarks are from a June 27, 2001 speech in Kuala Lumpur at a conference co-sponsored by *BusinessWeek*.

12   United Nations Development Program, *op.cit.*, p. 31.

13   *Ibid.*, p. 40.

14   The Uri Dadush quote is from the World Bank web page press release on *Global Economic Prospects and the Developing Countries 2001*, Washington, D.C., The World Bank, 2001, at: http://wbln0018.worldbank.org/news/pressrelease.nsf/Press+Releases/ 999119E933F6B6CA852569AC004C4BDF?OpenDocument. The data on tariffs is from the press release and the World Bank report, especially pp. 65–67.

15   For an incisive look at the promise that working in an export factory holds, see Dexter Roberts, "The Great Migration", *BusinessWeek*, December 11, 2000. For a very different case, one that spotlights abuses in a southern Chinese factory that produced handbags for Wal-Mart, see Dexter Roberts and Aaron Bernstein, "A Life of Fines and Beatings", *BusinessWeek*, October 2, 2000.

16   *Foreign Policy, op.cit.*, pp. 41–42, 51.

17   For a good summary of recent research, see *Global Economic Prospects, op.cit.*, pp. 88–93.

CHAPTER 3

Enter the Dragon

It was a moment leaders in Beijing and Washington had been anticipating for more than a decade. As dusk turned to night on a cold and windy November afternoon in Beijing, Chinese President Jiang Zemin and USTR Charlene Barshefsky shook hands for photographers in Hanyuandian Hall, a room tucked inside the Zhongnanhai leadership compound in the city's center. With its huge painting of Chinese mountain scenery, elaborate porcelain vases and exquisite calligraphy, the grand hall is one of the finest of the 275 rooms that make up this stunning complex in the heart of the capital.

Qing dynasty emperors once entertained princes and dukes in this room, making it a fitting backdrop for Jiang and Barshefsky to celebrate a Sino-US bilateral trade agreement that promised to bring some of the world's longest-running trade negotiations closer to a conclusion. It was a brief moment of unalloyed good feeling in the Sino-US relationship, a time of celebration and triumph. Jiang laughed repeatedly during the 10-minute Zhongnanhai photo-op, first pumping Barshefsky's hand and then in English urging "everybody" in the American delegation to shake his hand. The hurriedly arranged meeting on November 15, 1999 occurred just half an hour after Barshefsky had finished six days of grueling negotiations with Shi Guangsheng, China's Minister of Foreign Trade and Economic Cooperation (MOFTEC), to hammer out what the two sides said was a final bilateral agreement for China to join the WTO. The talks had come to a successful result thanks in part to last-minute behind-the-scenes intervention by Premier Zhu Rongji. Now, Jiang's appearance with Barshefsky underscored the president's support for economic reformers like Zhu and their attempts to transform China's economy. Given the events that had occurred during the previous seven months, when both WTO membership and economic reform faced occasionally fierce internal opposition, Jiang's presence sent an important signal to the country.[1]

Certainly, the deal provided many of the benefits US companies had long been after. Foreign companies could own 49% of local telecommunications and Internet firms, with the share rising to 50% two years after accession. Agriculture tariffs would be cut to 14.5%, on average, and China agreed not to subsidize agricultural exports. Foreign banks would see geographic restrictions on their business eliminated and bigger opportunities for a variety of businesses, including automobile financing. Hollywood celebrated a wider opening of the film market to its movies, one that would allow 20 foreign films a year to be shown in China.

The US also successfully negotiated a number of restrictions designed to keep Chinese exports, especially clothing exports, from being too successful too quickly in the US market. Although the US, along with the rest of the WTO countries, will do away with onerous restrictions on textile and apparel products (the so-called MFA or ATC regime) in 2005, the US will keep quotas and, in a place for Chinese products for four years after accession. US companies also worried about hidden subsidies in China's planned economy, so they won the right to classify China as a non-market economy for 15 years. This provision makes it much easier for aggrieved US companies to win dumping cases, because they can use imputed prices of production (drawn from other countries) to prove that a company is selling something at below its cost of production.

Here is how the USTR presented the highlights of the agreement's outline following the conclusion of the talks. It's worth noting both the broad general concessions by China embodied in the agreement as well as the very product-specific concessions in areas such as film and soy.

This agreement provides significant access for US agriculture, industrial products and services. China will reduce both tariff and non-tariff barriers to industrial goods and farm products. The agreement contains strong provisions to address import surges and unfair trade practices. China has agreed to take specific actions to ensure fair treatment for businesses operating in China. These include limits on technology-transfer requirements, offsets and export performance requirements.

Some specific examples from the agreement include:
- *China will cut duties from an overall average of 22.1% to 17%.*
- *China will make even greater reductions on agricultural items of particular interest to the United States.*
- *China will establish large and increasing tariff-rate quotas*

> *for wheat, corn, rice and cotton, with a substantial share reserved for private trade.*

- *State trading for soy oil will be phased out.*

- *China will eliminate export subsidies.*

- *American companies can provide auto financing.*

- *New access for US companies, including banks, insurance companies and telecommunications businesses.*

- *Distribution rights for US exporters.*

- *Improved access for computer services, business consulting, accounting, advertising and financial information services.*

- *Increased imports of foreign films, on a revenue-sharing basis, to at least 20 films per year.*

- *In textiles, the US and China agreed on appropriate measures to avoid market disruptions during and after the phase-out of current quotas.[2]*

Barshefsky lauded the deal: "The agreement itself is absolutely comprehensive," she said while meeting journalists later that day. "It covers all goods, all services, all of agriculture. It covers a variety of rules with respect to import surges, technology transfers, state trading enterprises, and high dumping, investing, subsidies and other issues ... This is just an extremely comprehensive and a very, very strong agreement."

Despite the ebullience of Barshefsky's characterization of the agreement as "comprehensive and ... very, very strong", it turned out to be neither. The US and China went back to the negotiating table repeatedly for another year-and-a-half to thrash out details of areas ranging from insurance to agriculture. Finally, in early June 2001, during the George W. Bush administration, Barshefsky's successor,

Robert Zoellick, reached another bilateral agreement with China. After a bargaining session that lasted until three o'clock on the morning of June 8, 2001, Minister Shi Guangsheng and Zoellick capped four days of negotiations in Shanghai with a deal. This time there were no public handshakes, no press conference, no confident expressions that this was a comprehensive agreement, just a press release put out by the Office of the USTR the following day.

Barely two months had passed since a crippled US spy plane landed on China's Hainan Island after a mid-air collision with a Chinese fighter plane that killed the Chinese pilot and plunged Sino-US relations to their lowest point since the North Atlantic Treaty Organization (NATO) bombing of China's embassy in Belgrade two years earlier. Since Shi's agreement with Barshefsky, the two sides had wrangled over, among other things, insurance, retail distribution and China's subsidies for its farmers. Although the US had won some concessions, the delay of two years had slowed reform in China and denied US businesses the opportunities that would come with China's WTO membership. For example, US banks waited an extra two years before they could open additional branches as further market-opening measures were put on hold until WTO accession was formalized. Foreign bankers weren't the only ones who were unhappy. Even reform-minded Chinese bankers fretted at the delay. The seemingly interminable wrangling over what in the end amounted to very little in the way of substantive changes underscored both how closely domestic politics are bound up with WTO accession negotiations and the need to explore ways of reforming the accession procedures.

JOINING THE CLUB: THE WTO ACCESSION PROCESS

In theory, China's 15-year odyssey to join the world trade body shouldn't have taken so long. WTO accession is, in its simplest form, a two-step process. First, the applicant must negotiate bilateral concession agreements with each current WTO member that requests such agreement. These bilateral agreements are then used as the basis to write an overall accession agreement that is approved by the entire WTO membership, known as the General Council. In keeping with the fundamental free-trade principle that one country cannot be favored over another, the most favorable offer made to one country must be offered to all as part of the accession agreement.

The bilateral agreements contain the applicant's commitment to each of these individual members with regard to market access for specific products. An important issue is agreement on tariffs. Although there may be a general commitment to lower average tariffs to a certain level, binding tariff rates must then be assigned to individual goods. These are typically negotiated for thousands of items with dominant trading partners. This is an often tedious and arcane task. Imports of, for example, whole soybeans, processed soybean meal and soybean oil could fall under different tariff rates.

Contentious and time-consuming as tariff negotiations can be, in many ways this is the easy part of trade negotiations. Although the WTO is working toward the ideal of making tariffs the only barrier to trade, the reality is that trade is riddled with all sorts of non-tariff arrangements, ranging from quotas to health and safety standards. Where there are non-tariff barriers, such as quotas on the amount of a product that can be imported, agreement must be reached on these as well. Typically, prospective members are pressured to eliminate (and must promise not to re-introduce) non-tariff measures such as quotas, licensing requirements, permits or notification requirements.

Countries can also hide behind pseudo-scientific trade barriers as well. Back in the 1980s, one Japanese official famously contended that Japanese people had different intestines from Westerners and, thus, that foreign beef imports should be restricted. It's to do away with these sorts of barriers that the WTO has adopted an agreement on Technical Barriers to Trade (TBT). The TBT Agreement encourages countries to accept internationally recognized tests in order to prevent the application of unilateral standards. After all, the decision to accept — or not accept — another country's standards can have a huge impact. If China were to decide to accept, for example, US Food and Drug Administration approval for pharmaceutical drugs as sufficient to sell a product in China, it could have a dramatic impact on foreign pharmaceutical makers. There's a growing trend for countries to accept each other's tests, so as to reduce costs and encourage trade. For example, there is a mutual recognition pact between the US and the European Union in electronics equipment, among other areas.

The bilateral agreements also include the terms of market entry for corporations, a services agreement, and other commitments in accordance with the existing Uruguay Round framework that governs trade talks. As noted in Chapter 2, one of the main changes in the world trading order, beginning with the Uruguay Round, is the inclusion of services in trade talks. This has been very important in the case of China. For example, US auto makers sought and eventually won the right to provide financing for their cars as well as the right to import and sell the cars — activities that had been prohibited. Financial services (insurance, banking and securities) and telecommunications services were major areas of contention. Naturally, these new areas add to complexity and thus contributed to prolonging China's accession talks.

Collectively, the members requesting bilateral agreements are referred to as an "accession working party". In the case of China, a full 37 countries requested bilateral agreements. The high number of bilateral negotiations reflected, quite naturally, concern that this emerging giant would have an unsettling impact on the world trading system. Each of the countries with which China conducted separate negotiations wanted its specific concerns met before it would agree to China's membership. Negotiations with the US were by far the most difficult and comprehensive. But China also had tough talks with the European Union. Like those with the US, an initial agreement (in the case of the EU, in May 2000) was followed by continuing disputes which were only resolved finally in mid-2001. But even after the US and the EU had concluded bilateral agreements with China, Mexico remained a holdout until just before final approval of China's accession. Mexico was concerned that its low-end manufacturing industries would be swamped by China's. Indeed, this is a significant concern that resonates throughout Latin America.

Once all the bilateral protocols are agreed, they must be codified and synthesized into the protocol of accession. The arrangements made in the bilateral concession agreements become multilateral — or available to all members — through the protocol. The bilateral agreements are incorporated into a schedule of commitments that is sent with the protocol, along with a report from the working party, to the WTO General Council for approval. Finally, a two-thirds majority of the General Council must approve the application of a new member.

In essence, the protocol outlines the applicant's current trade laws and policies, while noting the differences between that regime and the inclusiveness of GATT/WTO requirements. The protocol contains the procedures for the applicant to adjust its policies to meet these requirements. For a more concrete discussion of what this will involve, see the discussion on the administrative and legal reforms specified by the draft of the protocol in Chapter 5.

Some applicants want the protocol to indicate their status as a developing country to enable them to take advantage of the so-called Special and Differential (S&D) treatment that allows developing countries some additional breathing room as they implement policies that make them fully compliant with WTO status. Not surprisingly, China argued strongly for developing-country status. Though it's rather far-fetched to imagine that China is anything other than a developing country, the US and other developed countries felt that letting China enjoy developing-country status could seriously distort the WTO and, perhaps, the entire world trading system. Developing-country status, in its broadest form, would have required other countries to grant China additional benefits. But China wouldn't be obliged to reciprocate, so it could have made preferential trade deals. China also would have been allowed to keep its existing non-tariff barriers on imports and to pursue protectionist policies as a way of preserving favored local industries.[3]

As negotiations wore on during the 1990s, China ceded on most of these points. But it refused to give ground on agriculture, citing the 900-million-strong rural population, more than one-third of whom are farmers. The US worried that allowing China to join as a developing country, which would allow markedly higher subsidies, could result in a flood of exports and be extremely disruptive to the world agricultural market. At least as important, increased Chinese subsidies for agriculture would undercut American farmers' attempts to export to China. The fight over whether or not China was eligible for this developing-country status is yet another reminder of the intense politicization of the accession process.

China wanted to have the freedom afforded developing countries to subsidize farmers up to 10% of the value of production. The US argued that because China was both one of the world's largest agricultural producers, with some $250 billion in annual production, and a highly competitive one in some areas, support should be capped at the 5% level that developed countries are allowed. China argued that it clearly was a developing country and that it wouldn't surrender a privilege that was due it, given its embryonic stage of economic development.

In the talks between Shi and Zoellick in June 2001 the two sides agreed on an 8.5% level, or about $21.5 billion at the then-current level of production. China also agreed that the 8.5% would refer both to the overall level of subsidy and the level of subsidy that can be given to any particular product, so subsidies couldn't be shoveled into particular areas. In a far-reaching concession, China also agreed to certain restrictions on how the subsidy is calculated that normally wouldn't apply to developing countries by waiving its right to have many rural infrastructure improvements excluded from the 8.5% limit. As a developing country, China could have given unlimited support for agricultural and rural development programs, such as investment subsidies. Although these sorts of subsidies were a paltry $156 million when the agreement was signed, the US worried that "China has both the historical experience and infrastructure to provide such support, since these were the kind of programs China often used under central planning".[4] Given that China only subsidizes agriculture to the tune of less than 2% annually, this was, above all, a political battle. Some developing countries were unhappy with China's concession, worrying that this could be the first step of a broader US-led drive to limit agricultural subsidies in developing countries.

Normally, accession negotiations should be completed as soon as possible to afford the applicant the chance to participate in new trade negotiations and agreements. If the applicants can take part in a new round of trade talks, they have the opportunity to influence the final outcome. If not, there is a greater chance that the applicants will be burdened by additional commitments over which they have no say. That was certainly the case with China. One reason China originally pushed to join in the early 1990s was so that it could count as a founding member of the WTO, which opened its doors at the beginning of 1995. Besides providing a chance to shape a new trade round, WTO membership would shield China from unilateral trade sanctions. The US was particularly vocal in threatening these sanctions. During most of the 1990s, it conducted an annual debate on whether or not to strip China of its MFN status. The message from Washington was simple: we can use trade as a weapon. Without WTO membership, China had no effective protection against this threat.

THE LONG MARCH TO GENEVA

The triumphal handshake between Jiang Zemin and Charlene Barshefsky came just seven months after President Bill Clinton had rejected an almost identical agreement offered by Premier Zhu Rongji. As Zhu set off from Beijing in early April 1999, his trip to the US appeared to be a well-calculated risk. Clinton had written three letters to Jiang between November 1998 and February 1999 expressing hope that a WTO deal could be concluded quickly. In January 1999, Zhu had told Federal Reserve Chairman Alan Greenspan that China was ready to make substantial concessions. After that, both US Deputy Treasury Secretary Lawrence H. Summers and Secretary of State Madeleine Albright had made trips to Beijing that included WTO discussions. And President Jiang Zemin strongly backed Zhu's trip.[5]

On the weekend of April 4–5, as Zhu readied himself for his trip to the United States, Clinton huddled with his advisors. Clinton's foreign policy team, including Albright, Barshefsky and National Security Advisor Samuel Berger, wanted to conclude a deal, one that by general agreement was "better for American businesses than any had dared hope only a few months earlier".[6] But Clinton's domestic policy team — Treasury Secretary Robert Rubin, National Economic Council head Gene Sperling and domestic political advisor John Podesta — contended that any agreement would need additional provisions to satisfy US labor unions and industries that could be hit hard by Chinese companies. Clinton backed his domestic advisors and told the USTR team to ask for more protection against import surges, in particular for textiles.

On the morning of April 7, Clinton said that it would be wrong to walk away from a good deal. Indeed, Zhu's offer was a stunner, providing for wide openings in areas ranging from agriculture to manufactured goods to services. But during a two-and-a-half-hour meeting with Zhu at the White House that same night, Clinton did exactly what he had promised not to do — he walked away from a good deal.

The following day, in an attempt to soften the sting of failure, the USTR hurriedly put out a statement lauding the broad market gains that resulted from the negotiations. Tellingly, the USTR's Barshefsky noted that "the scope of issues involved in these negotiations is unparalleled outside of a multilateral Round. There are more than 5,000 tariff line items and complex interlocking issues from national treatment to distribution rights which we have addressed here to ensure fair treatment and enforceable rights for US goods, services, and agricultural providers. The Leaders noted that we have reached agreement concerning market access for agricultural and industrial goods as well as a wide range of services sectors, but that certain differences remain to be resolved in banking, including auto finance, securities, and audio-visual services." At the urging of US business, Clinton tried to repair the damage with a telephone call to Zhu in New York on April 13. The US president limply promised to do what he could to get China into the WTO by year-end. But the damage was done.[7]

To compound the trouble the US had caused for Zhu, the USTR posted on its website what it contended was the Chinese offer. Although the USTR apparently hoped to lock in the Chinese, this had the effect of galvanizing opposition to the offer among many Chinese ministries and domestic industries, many or most of whom had never seen Zhu's proposals. The USTR's questionable decision to post the content of these bilateral talks on its website came perilously close to seriously undercutting Zhu's authority at home and dramatically slowing the whole reform process.

Throughout his nine-day, six-city tour of the US, the premier surprised audiences with his self-deprecating humor and confident, no-nonsense speaking style. In Los Angeles, he joked that the Chinese Army would consider writing "Made in China, not in USA" on the side of its missiles, making light of accusations that China had stolen US nuclear weapons secrets. In Washington, Zhu and Clinton held an unexpectedly lengthy press conference, during which Zhu answered questions from the audience spontaneously, in marked contrast to the carefully scripted statements of most Chinese leaders. In Denver, he visited the Denver Broncos' training camp and showed off his football passing skills. In Chicago, Zhu accepted a 1500-pound Angus bull genetically engineered to produce high-quality beef. Capping his trip, Zhu engaged in a question-and-answer session with an audience at the Massachusetts Institute of Technology in Boston.

Not since Deng Xiaoping's famous tour of the US in 1979, when the pint-sized Szechuan native donned a Texas cowboy hat at a Houston rodeo, had Americans been so besotted by a Chinese leader. Zhu's visit did much to clear the post-Tiananmen animosity and suspicion with which many Americans regarded China. Here was a man who talked the language of markets, a Communist Chinese leader America could, literally, do business with. The irony was obvious: business had prolonged the talks with its pressure on successive US administrations. Now that the US corporate community had a WTO deal it could live with, the trade talks had become so politicized that the Clinton White House couldn't sign an agreement for fear of a backlash from labor.

Clinton's failure to seize the moment soon appeared costly. On May 7, 1999, a month after Zhu met Clinton at the White House, a NATO warplane with an American pilot bombed China's embassy in Belgrade, killing three Chinese. The US insisted that the bombing was an accident, the result of some old maps that had inaccurate information. Not surprisingly, many Chinese rejected the explanation. How could the world's undisputed military and economic superpower erroneously target a sovereign embassy with its "smart" bombs? The fact that the strike was neatly surgical, primarily destroying the part of the complex that contained sensitive communications equipment, only added to the doubts about the US explanation.

Certainly, the Chinese public refused to believe that it was an innocent mistake. Protesters took to the streets in Beijing and several other cities in the largest demonstrations the Chinese capital had seen since the pro-democracy protests of June 1989. US Ambassador James Sasser was trapped in the US Embassy in Beijing for several days as angry protestors hurled firebombs and smashed windows. His wife narrowly escaped from the embassy residence by climbing out a bedroom window. A mob trashed the US consulate in the inland city of Chengdu. Chinese authorities allowed the demonstrations to go ahead and policemen watched impassively as demonstrators attacked US facilities. Vice President Hu Jintao went on television and attacked what he called a "criminal act" by US-led NATO forces. Hu noted that "students and other citizens" were protesting outside US diplomatic facilities in Beijing, Shanghai, Guangzhou, Chengdu and Shenyang. "The Chinese government firmly supports and protects, in accordance with the law, all legal protest activities." The Chinese harked back to the Boxer Rebellion nearly a century earlier, when an eight-nation allied force invaded the country. Indeed, as bilateral relations plummeted, a US diplomat expressed private concerns that the incident could have the same damaging effect on China's relations with the outside world as the Boxer Rebellion had had, if the situation wasn't handled correctly.

After the failed mission in April and the bombing in May, there was little hope of moving forward on WTO accession. Not surprisingly, most of the domestic Chinese criticism focused on Premier Zhu Rongji, although President Jiang Zemin was also attacked by nationalistic leaders for being soft on the United States. Zhu was savaged as a "traitor" and accused of selling out the country. Some compared his package to Japan's "21 demands" in 1915 that aimed to reduce China to a colony. Scholar Joseph Fewsmith even contends that the broader Sino-US relationship, perhaps even China's commitment to an outward-looking, market-oriented economy, hung in the balance during a precarious seven-month period. That may be too strong a view, but there's little doubt that Zhu and Jiang were under tremendous pressure from those who wanted a more cautious approach to liberalization and economic opening.

There can be little better illustration of the degree to which WTO accession can be a game of power politics as much as a simple trade agreement than the way in which the Clinton administration snubbed Zhu with their rejection of the Chinese offer. Yet it accepted virtually the same offer less than six months later. Indeed, in some respects, the Zhu offer, at least as posted on the USTR website, contained provisions that were better than those ultimately agreed to. A notable case was telecommunications, where, in April, Zhu offered foreign companies the right to own up to 51% of Chinese telecoms companies; in November the US agreed to accept a 50% cap. To give the US negotiators their due, the November agreement did resolve some issues that had been ambiguous in Zhu's offer. These included Chinese acceptance of US safeguard and anti-dumping provisions, as well as market access in China for foreign banking, securities and entertainment companies.

In the end, the setback to reform and to Sino-US relations fortunately proved limited to a matter of months. Although WTO talks were suspended for a time, the two sides sat down again in August. Having stepped to the brink, China and the US quickly repaired the damage and came to a preliminary agreement in November. Among other reasons, China hoped to be part of the new round of trade talks scheduled to kick off as early as the WTO ministerial meeting in Seattle at the end of November. As discussed earlier, that meeting was a debacle. China's delay in accession was to be cost-free, at least as far as its involvement in another round was concerned.

❧   ❧   ❧

The former Republic of China was one of 23 original members who banded together to sign the General Agreement on Tariffs and Trade on October 30, 1947. The other founding parties made up what today would be a grouping that would agree on very little. They included Burma, Cuba, South Africa and the United States. As noted, the spirit behind GATT was that which had animated the Bretton Woods institutions, the International Monetary Fund and the World Bank, which were founded in the aftermath of World War II as a way of building international cooperation and preventing the dangerous unilateral actions that had led to two world wars in less than half a century.

China's membership in GATT didn't last long. On October 1, 1949, Chinese Communist Party leader Mao Zedong proclaimed victory in his battle with the Kuomintang – dominated government of Generalissimo Chiang Kai-shek and declared the establishment of the People's Republic of China. Little more than five months later, on March 6, 1950, the Nationalist government on Taiwan withdrew from GATT. In 1965, Taiwan requested observer status in GATT, which it was granted after protests from the communist world. But Taiwan lost its GATT status in 1971, at the same time as it was expelled from the United Nations and the seat given to the People's Republic of China.

Logically, it would have made sense for China to have sought GATT membership in 1971, at least as an observer, when it wrested the United Nations seat away from Taiwan. This would have allowed it to take part in two subsequent trade rounds, the Tokyo Round and the Uruguay Round. Also, at that time the threshold for membership was lower, in part because GATT commitments weren't legally binding.

So China almost certainly could have gotten in very quickly. But China was preoccupied with the internal upheaval and top-level factional struggles that accompanied the Cultural Revolution (1966–76) and the declining health of Chairman Mao. Moreover, China remained resolutely anti-capitalist at the time and its trade volumes were minuscule, so entering a world trade body made little sense.

After economic reforms began in 1978, China gradually began joining international economic-related organizations. As noted above, in 1980 it successfully applied to join the World Bank and the IMF. That same year, China applied for participation as a non-voting observer at GATT. Chinese officials began to attend courses in Geneva that GATT ran for interested parties — members and non-members alike. GATT granted China observer status in November 1982, allowing Beijing to attend the GATT Ministerial Council meetings planning the terms of negotiation for subsequent trade rounds, and China participated in the Uruguay Round negotiations as an observer. In 1983, it became a party to the Multi-Fiber Arrangement. The following year it became a permanent observer at the GATT Ministerial Council.

China, in other words, had already established a rather lengthy track record at GATT when it formally applied for "the restoration of China's signatory state status" to GATT on July 11, 1986.[8] It hoped to avoid the lengthy accession process by asking GATT to give it back the seat that the defeated Nationalist regime had withdrawn from in 1950, much as it had taken over the UN seat. As the subsequent 15-year negotiations were to prove, the strategy was unsuccessful. Although China never formally withdrew its request to simply resume the Chinese seat, its claim had died a quiet death by the mid-1990s as the Chinese proved unable to circumvent the normal accession process. In response to China's request to re-join GATT, the organization established a "Working Party on China's Status as a Contracting Party" in March 1987.

Not surprisingly, given the difficult transition China was making from a planned economy (and a poor, largely agricultural one at that), even agreeing on what would be included in the negotiations was complex and difficult. Because of China's sheer size, and the rapid strides it was making as an exporter of manufactured goods, GATT members were determined not to let China in on easy terms. The mid- and late 1980s were a time of mounting trade tensions, as rich GATT members such as the US and much of Europe sparred with the rapidly rising economies of East Asia, especially Japan, Taiwan and South Korea. All three of these fast-growing countries were accused of pursuing neo-mercantilist trade policies, of stoking powerful export machines while keeping their markets largely closed to imports. And it looked like China might be the next, biggest trading power. Hong Kong manufacturers were in the midst of setting up thousands of factories in the Pearl River delta, factories that by the mid-1990s would employ some six million workers and help make southern China one of the most important low-end manufacturing centers in the world. If China were permitted to enter the WTO on easy terms, some GATT members feared, it could undercut the organization's integrity as a trade-promoting body. The unspoken fear was that more than a billion low-wage Chinese could decimate untold industries in the developed world.

When formal negotiations with China began, they included the following issues:

- China's tariff barriers, which, at the time, averaged 35%, far exceeding those of existing GATT members.
- China's non-tariff barriers, such as the lack of transparency and the absence of uniformity in China's customs requirements and trade laws.
- Market access for foreign financial services companies, such as banks, insurance companies and securities houses.
- Government subsidies for the state-owned enterprises that dominated the economy.
- The lack of convertibility for China's currency, the *yuan*.
- Chinese labor standards.
- Enforcement of intellectual-property laws, which at the time was virtually non-existent.

Talks progressed slowly and the aim of GATT membership often seemed more like a slogan than a serious policy commitment. Top Chinese policy makers showed little commitment to GATT membership. For example, in a bilateral meeting between Chinese and Thai officials in the late 1980s, the Minister of Foreign Trade and Economic Cooperation, Wu Yi, didn't even bring up the subject of GATT membership. (Wu's ministry was responsible for accession negotiations to GATT.) China had already been granted Most Favored Nation status by its major trading partners, and GATT had no binding way of settling trade disputes. Moreover, the US had not yet threatened to use MFN treatment as a political tool (something it couldn't do to GATT member countries), so there was little obvious advantage for China in joining. Indeed, accession would have required it to make a number of concessions and to overhaul its internal economy.

The violent suppression of pro-democracy protests in and around Beijing's Tiananmen Square on June 4, 1989 slowed down the trade talks even further. World Bank loans to China were frozen. Economic and diplomatic ties with much of the world were put on ice. China turned inward for several years, more concerned with domestic stability and keeping economic reforms at home on track than with major international initiatives. Moreover, the crackdown raised doubts in the developed world about China's commitment to reform and its ability to meet the sort of requirements that GATT demanded.

Making matters worse, economic stresses kept rising as China's international power increased. The US was particularly alarmed at growing intellectual-property rights violations, as well as opaque government procedures and policies on trade. Rising textile shipments from China also added to tensions. In October 1991, the USTR initiated an investigation into Chinese market barriers under Section 301 of the Trade Act of 1974, mainly because of the lack of transparency in China's trade laws and administrative rulings. In October 1992, after a year of negotiations, USTR Ambassador Mickey Kantor and Minister Wu Yi signed a memorandum of understanding on market access. It covered issues such as transparency, quantitative restrictions on imports, import substitution, standards and testing, tariffs, export restrictions and market access. The US agreed that it would "staunchly support" China's entry into GATT and agreed to drop a number of investigations into unfair trade practices. Soon after this, though, additional Sino-US disputes emerged in areas ranging from allegations that prison labor and child labor were used for Chinese export products, to narrower trade issues such as financial services and telecommunications liberalization. Disagreement over whether or not China could enjoy developing-country status also remained unresolved.

Despite the ever-broader set of issues that the US and other trading partners insisted on discussing, China's determination to join the WTO only grew. As China's economic integration with the rest of the world increased, and as exports played an ever-more important role in its economic growth, the benefits of GATT's protections became more pronounced. And the potential cost of remaining outside of the GATT regime grew, particularly after the US Congress began to engage in an annual debate over whether or not it should revoke China's MFN trade status in response to human-rights violations. The debate over revoking MFN was initiated in response to the suppression of the Tiananmen protests, but it soon became the highlight of critics' attempts to spotlight China's abuses. Finally, rivalry with Taiwan played an important role in China's stepped-up interest in GATT entry. In 1990, Taiwan began its own effort to rejoin GATT. In September 1992, GATT set up a working group to consider China's application and granted observer status to what was known as Chinese Taipei.

The GATT negotiations with China occurred against the backdrop of a trade relationship that was both fraught with difficulties yet growing rapidly, above all with the United States. Chinese exports to the US surged from a paltry $3.1 billion in 1984 to almost $38 billion in 1994. At the same time, US exports only increased from $3 billion to $8.8 billion. Against the backdrop of large and persistent trade deficits with other East Asian countries, Washington's patience at what it saw as Chinese recalcitrance on trade issues wore dangerously thin.

China's unwillingness to protect US intellectual-property rights (IPR) was a particular source of concern to Washington. In 1992, the two sides had signed an agreement on intellectual property. The agreement had little effect and Chinese shops and street merchants were filled with increasing numbers of pirated CDs, movies and software. Indeed, as much as 94% of computer software in China was pirated, according to a US government report in 1994. Piracy rates in many parts of China hit nearly 100% for US CDs, video games, videos, books and movies. Making matters worse, the two years following the 1992 IPR agreement saw pirate factories begin to export on a large scale. In 1994, the US contended that 29 CD and laser disc factories in China had a production capacity of 75 million CDs for a market that could absorb only five million CDs annually. "Despite repeated requests, China has taken no significant action to stop infringing activities in these factories," the US complained.

On February 4, 1995, USTR Mickey Kantor ordered 100% tariffs on $1.1 billion-worth of Chinese goods in retaliation against Chinese factories making pirated products and the country's inability to protect US computer software, pharmaceuticals, agricultural and chemical products, movies, books and trademarks from rip-offs. The hit list included everything from answering machines to jewelry boxes to children's bicycles to surf boards, and constituted the largest trade retaliation ever announced by the US.

The USTR cited numerous examples to back up its contention that China was a massive IPR pirate. A USTR report noted that industry representatives visiting the Shenfei Laser Optical Systems Co. in Shenzhen, just over the border from Hong Kong, found copies of more than

30 US movies for sale. Salesroom staff "bragged that the pirated copies were being exported to South Korea, Taiwan, Singapore, Malaysia and Thailand, and that they were looking for new export markets all the time". Because of limits on the number of foreign films that could be imported, *Terminator II* couldn't be legally imported into China. Thanks to the knock-offs, however, the movie was, in the words of the USTR, a "blockbuster hit" in thousands of China's video cinemas.[9]

The threat of trade retaliation at last spurred Chinese action and kicked off an intensive set of negotiations that continued until the sanctions were set to begin. On February 26, the very day the punitive tariffs were to take effect, the US and China wrapped up a round of intensive negotiations and concluded a landmark IPR agreement. Just the previous night Chinese authorities had raided the Shenfei factory in Shenzhen, which the US regarded as one of the most notorious pirate factories. More important, China vowed to take steps to prohibit the export of pirated products and to implement a Special Enforcement Period during which the government would target large-scale manufacturers and distributors of illegal products. China also promised to make a number of long-term structural changes to limit IPR violations. These ranged from creating a customs service enforcement system modeled on the US Customs Service, to special working groups at the central, local and provincial levels, to increased import rights for US music and movies.[10]

Although friction remained, in June 1996 Acting USTR Charlene Barshefsky declared that China had reached a critical mass in IPR enforcement and that no sanctions would be imposed. Barshefsky noted that China had closed

15 pirate CD factories with an estimated production capacity of 30–50 million units a year. Barshefsky made her statement just before the annual vote on MFN status that had become a ritual test of opposition to Beijing. Throughout the jousting over IPR that took the two nations to the edge of a trade war in 1995–96, the WTO-membership question took a back seat to the trade disputes.

Frosty Sino-US relations during the early years of the Clinton administration also acted to slow accession. During the 1992 presidential campaign, Clinton caught the public mood with his attack on the "butchers" of Beijing. The following year, the US Congress and the US Olympic Committee opposed Beijing's bid for the 2000 Summer Olympics, a bid that China lost narrowly to Sydney. The opposition angered many ordinary Chinese and marked the beginning of a subtle shift away from the pro-US sentiments that had prevailed among most Chinese since the 1970s. Then official relations deteriorated badly in 1995–96. First, in the summer of 1995, the White House and the US State Department bungled Taiwan President Lee Teng-hui's visit to the United States. After repeatedly insisting to the Chinese that it wouldn't allow the Taiwanese leader to speak at Cornell University, his alma mater, the Administration abruptly shifted course in the face of Congressional support for the visit, and only belatedly informed the Chinese.

Chinese leaders, who are extremely sensitive to any move that appears to legitimize Taiwan's government, retaliated with a series of live missile tests in the waters around Taiwan in March 1996, on the eve of the island's presidential election. The US sent two aircraft carrier battle groups to steam through the Taiwan Strait as a show of force. At times during 1996–97, signals emanating from Beijing suggested that China was losing interest in WTO membership. In a conversation during this period, trade minister Wu Yi remarked that China's longest war with a foreign power had lasted only eight years, but that it had already taken China more than ten years to battle through the WTO accession process — and no end was in sight.

Fortunately, Sino-US relations improved dramatically, beginning with a state visit that Jiang Zemin made to the US in October 1997. China agreed to buy $3 billion-worth of Boeing jets and Clinton lifted a 12-year ban on the sale of US nuclear-power-plant technology to China. China, in turn, agreed that it would end the supply of nuclear technology to Iran, among other countries. On that visit, Jiang announced that China would sign the Information Technology Agreement, which will eliminate tariffs on a wide range of technology imports by 2005. These moves came against other signs of progress. Shortly after Jiang's visit, USTR general counsel Susan Esserman said that her office saw "real progress" in China's trade practices. She cited China's agreement to phase in trading rights within three years of WTO entry; to adopt the TRIPS (intellectual property) regime immediately on accession; to eliminate export subsidies for agricultural products; to end a dual-pricing system; and to bring more transparency and fairness into the trading process. Nonetheless, Esserman said the US still had "particular concern" about market access in the services sector, including telecommunications, financial services, distribution services and professional services.

The two presidents met again later that year at the Vancouver APEC summit at the end of November, amidst what seemed to be a growing momentum for serious talks as a result of Clinton's impending 10-day state visit to China slated for June 1998. But both the EU and the US continued to contend that China's offer on services wasn't good enough. Trade minister Wu Yi told her EU counterpart, Sir Leon Brittan, that it was "unfair and unrealistic to expect China to achieve quickly what developed countries have achieved over 100 to 200 years". Shortly after that, Deputy USTR Richard Fisher contended: "We don't have a basis to assess their [the Chinese] seriousness of proceeding toward WTO accession." Although a visit to Beijing by Fisher's boss, Charlene Barshefsky, in April had gone well, Barshefsky seemingly changed her tune in the run-up to the summit, saying, "There's lots of talk, but China is not ready to walk the walk."[11]

The Chinese had to fight off a good deal of skepticism during this period because of worries that they had lost interest in the WTO due to a combination of the Asian financial crisis — which showed the dangers of a rapid opening of the financial services market — and the difficulties associated with reforming the domestic economy. Rising protests among laid-off workers and unhappy farmers alike had captured the attention of the Chinese leadership. The dramatic opening that WTO entry demanded naturally would be another shock and it seemed for a time as if conservatives in the leadership had won the argument to slow the pace of concessions.

For its part, the Clinton administration was on the defensive with regard to China. Clinton needed organized labor's support, but labor was opposed to China's WTO entry because of fears that it would mean the loss of US jobs to China's low-wage workers. At the same time, allegations of illegal campaign contributions by China-linked organizations and subsequent allegations of the Chinese theft of US nuclear secrets made it politically imperative that the Clinton administration be seen to be driving a tough bargain on China's entry to the WTO. During Clinton's visit to China in 1998, the two sides continued repairing what had often been a troubled relationship. In Shanghai, Clinton publicly embraced the Chinese "Three Nos" policy — no support for Taiwan's independence, for Taiwan's entry into the United Nations or for its entry into international organizations. This was the first time that a US president had publicly affirmed US support for this policy. Just as striking, Clinton spoke of "constructive, strategic partnership" between the two countries during an appearance at Beijing's Great Hall of the People. Although China didn't present an offer that the Americans found satisfactory in time to wrap anything up during the Clinton visit, the trip made the prospect for serious WTO negotiations better than at any time in several years.[12]

It was against this background that Zhu came to the US with his dramatic package. Even allowing for Jiang's backing for the trip, and the more positive signals that had come from senior US administration officials who were visiting Beijing, it was a gutsy trip to make. Zhu's offer far exceeded anything that had been offered previously, notably in areas like telecommunications. It was about as close as a trade negotiator ever gets to a knock-out bid. But Zhu's trip took place against the background of American ambivalence toward, even distrust of, China.

For all the distance that China had come since it had applied to join GATT almost 13 years earlier, US domestic concerns proved too high a hurdle to overcome. Next would come the embassy bombing and a fear that negotiations would be knocked off track for some time. That the talks weren't derailed and the two sides were able to shake hands on a deal — albeit prematurely — less than eight months later proved a triumph of leadership and a recognition that the relationship was too important to squander.

---

[1] The account of the Zhongnanhai photo-op was provided by Dexter Roberts, *BusinessWeek*'s Beijing bureau chief, who attended the ceremony.

[2] Office of the United States Trade Representative, "US China Sign Historic Trade Agreement", November 15, 1999, USTR website (www.ustr.gov). Citation: http://192.239.92.165/releases/1999/11/99-95.html. (See Appendix 1 for a fuller account of the Agreement).

[3] See Sean Leonard, *The Dragon Awakens: China's Long March to Geneva*, London, Cameron May, 1999, p. 19, for an account of what privileges China would enjoy if it joined as a developing nation.

[4] "USTR Releases Details on US-China Consensus on China's WTO Accession", USTR Press release, June 14, 2001, from the USTR website (http://192.239.92.165/releases/2001/06/01-38.htm). Here are some of the relevant provisions:

2. Article 6.4: China agreed to a "de minimis" exemption of 8.5%.

   •   Under a provision of the Agreement on Agriculture (Article 6.4), countries are permitted to exempt from calculation of their AMS any support that falls below a certain minimum or the de minimis level mentioned above.

   •   We sought a lower exemption for China because China is one of the world's largest agricultural producers (China's average annual agricultural production totals about $250 billion), and is a highly competitive producer of a number of agricultural products.

   •   In Shanghai, China agreed to a de minimis exemption of 8.5%, which means that China's subsidies will be capped at this amount, both for general support and for each specific product.

3. Article 6.2: China agreed to forgo recourse to this separate exemption.

   •   Article 6.2 of the Agreement on Agriculture permits developing countries an unlimited exemption for support for programs intended to encourage agricultural and rural development for resource-poor farmers, in particular investment subsidies programs, input subsidies programs, and programs for diversification from narcotic crops.

- Developed countries are not eligible for this separate exemption.
- Though China currently provides about $156 million-worth of these kinds of subsidies, it could increase such support dramatically in the future. China has both the historical experience and infrastructure to provide such support, since these were the kind of programs China often used under central planning.
- In Shanghai, China agreed to include subsidies provided for programs described in Article 6.2 in the calculation of its AMS. These subsidies will therefore be subject to the 8.5% cap.

4. Export Subsidies: China reaffirmed its 1997 multilateral commitment to forgo all export subsidies for agriculture.

⁵ The account of the 1999 WTO talks is largely based on the following sources: Joseph Fewsmith, "China and the WTO: The Politics Behind the Agreement", The National Bureau of Asian Research, November 1999 (at www.nbr.org); Leonard, *op.cit.*, pp. 143–54; Steven Mufson and Robert G. Kaiser, "Missed US-China Deal Looms Large", *Washington Post*, November 10, 1999. More generally, James Mann, *About Face*, New York, N.Y., Alfred A. Knopf, 1999, is an excellent source on the US-China relationship.

⁶ Fewsmith, *op.cit.*, p. 1.

⁷ "Statement of Ambassador Charlene Barshefsky Regarding Broad Market Access Gains Resulting from China WTO Negotiations", April 8, 1999 (http://192.239.92.165/releases/1999/04/99-34.html). See also "US-China Sign Bilateral Agriculture Agreement", April 10, 1999 (http://192.239.92.165/releases/1999/04/99-36.html).

⁸ Leonard, *op.cit.,* p. 15, n. 2.

⁹ Information on the February intellectual-property rights retaliation comes from the USTR website, "USTR Mickey Kantor Orders 100% Tariffs on More Than $1 Billion of Chinese Imports: Cites China's Failure to Protect US Intellectual Property" (http://192.239.92.165/releases/1995/02/95-08).

¹⁰ "United States and China Reach Accord on Protection of Intellectual Property Rights, Market Access", USTR website (http://192.239.92.165/releases/1995/02/95-12).

¹¹ The preceding section is substantially drawn from Leonard, *op.cit.*, pp. 106–16.

¹² For example, Joseph Fewsmith notes that the trip "… made serious negotiations possible, perhaps for the first time since 1994", *op.cit.*, p. 3.

CHAPTER 4

The Asia Puzzle

China's entry into the WTO will dramatically raise the stakes for its Asian neighbors and rivals. The increased certainty for business that goes with WTO membership should drive a new round of foreign direct investment in China and, after an initial period of disruption, a higher sustained growth rate. After WTO entry, China's investment environment will be codified in an international agreement that will protect foreign investors. And its trade status will no longer be questionable, subject to the whims of trading partners like the US, where politicians critical of China's human-rights record have repeatedly tried to curtail China's trading privileges. As a rising power, China's increased prominence will naturally mean economic dislocations for its neighbors. But how much of this is a threat and how much of it is an opportunity? Should its Asian neighbors welcome China's economic rise, of which the WTO marks a major milestone, or be afraid of it?

On the positive side of the ledger, the effect of an expanding China should buoy the region, driving big increases in trade and acting as a spur to broader economic reforms. In this scenario, the increased economic activity will stimulate trade, foreign direct investment and economies throughout the East Asian region. For example, Goldman Sachs' Hong Kong-based economist Fred Hu looks for import growth to accelerate from 7% to 12% annually after China joins the WTO. China's vast and increasingly international economy will pull in imports and become a locomotive of growth for the region. Given World Bank estimates that China will make up 40% of developing countries' import growth over the next 20 years, it seems obvious that its Asian neighbors should share powerfully in that growth. But regional growth will be uneven. To remain attractive in a region dominated by China, its neighbors will have to accelerate reforms. China's rise could even stimulate a competitive momentum for reform. Under this scenario, China's ascendancy would spur countries around the region to do everything from cleaning up financial systems and making them more market-oriented to cracking down on corruption as a way of improving their economic and social attractiveness in the face of competition from a large, fast-growing China.

The positive scenario holds that the trade-creating impact of China's WTO entry will more than offset the costs. Because China will dramatically increase imports of capital-intensive and other more sophisticated goods as part of the industrial upgrading that will follow WTO entry, the region's more developed economies such as Korea, Japan and Taiwan should be big winners. Producers of home appliances, steel and processed food will all benefit from a growing, more open China. Other beneficiaries of China's growth, if not specifically its WTO entry, will be the oil- and gas-producing countries of the region, such as Indonesia and Malaysia. That's because China is expected to account for much of the incremental demand in energy consumption in the developing world over the next decade.

A more pessimistic scenario holds that China's entry into the WTO could bolster the country's already formidable competitive position at the expense of the rest of the region. "Our biggest challenge is ... to secure a niche for ourselves as China swamps the world with her high-quality but cheaper products," Singapore Prime Minister Goh Chok Tong warned in a National Day speech in August 2001. "China's economy is potentially 10 times the size of Japan's. Just ask yourselves, how does Singapore compete against 10 post-war Japans all industrializing and exporting at the same time?"[1] Similar sentiments are heard throughout Asia. "What if China is the world's lowest-cost producer of everything?" wondered a mid-2001 economic research report from Tim Condon, a Hong Kong-based economist at ING Barings.[2] That additional competitiveness could feed on itself, diverting even more of the investment that might otherwise have gone to Southeast Asia. Under the gloomier scenario, much of China's rise will be at the cost of its neighbors' prosperity, as China wins the battle for foreign investment and for exports. Even giant India, which traditionally has had only modest economic ties, is steeling itself against a flood of Chinese exports that are threatening to eviscerate much of the country's low-end manufacturing industry. "China will be an engine for growth and a tremendous competitor, eating the grass from under other countries' feet," contends Claude Smadja, an advisor to the World Economic Forum.

Most foreign businessmen seem to be in the negative camp. A survey of expatriates in Asia in mid-2001 by the Hong Kong-based Political & Economic Risk Consultancy found that 61% of the respondents in the Philippines thought that WTO entry would hurt their business, while only 31% thought it would help. In Malaysia, 45% thought it would be a negative, while only 9% thought China's accession would help their business. In Vietnam, 83% thought it was a bad thing and only 6% felt it was good. In India, two-thirds felt it was bad and one-third thought it would have no impact. No one who responded to the survey in India thought that China's entry would be positive for their business.

Trade isn't a zero-sum game, of course; so even the pessimists concede that there will be benefits for Southeast Asia in China's WTO entry. And some of the political and business leaders in much of the region who profess concern at a more competitive China have started to take steps to respond. Given how long it will be until China is equivalent to 10 Japans, Goh's speech was designed to galvanize action. Goh's hope is that Singapore can move away from low-end manufacturing operations and into more sophisticated and profitable industries. Some countries, such as Thailand, are overhauling industries in preparation; others, such as Malaysia, are hoping that what they lose in foreign investment from other sources will be made up for by increased investment on the part of the Chinese. But we are among those concerned that Southeast Asia, in particular, will have a difficult time meeting the China challenge. China's WTO entry should become a catalyst for reform. To date, however, it's been little more than an excuse for hand-wringing. Meanwhile, plans for regional economic integration have slipped behind schedule as countries balk at the adjustment costs involved in opening their markets.

In any event, no matter how thorough the preparations,

the entry of China is bound to cause ripples throughout the region as companies and governments respond to an increasingly powerful competitor. Less-advanced countries, or countries that have to depend primarily on labor-intensive industries (especially Southeast Asian countries such as Laos, Vietnam, Burma and Cambodia), will have to move rapidly or risk being hurt. Even far-off Mexico is concerned that low wages and relatively high productivity in China will undercut the advantages it enjoys thanks to its proximity to the US market. Flextronics, a prominent contract manufacturer for big name-brand electronics companies, is already moving manufacturing from Mexico to China, where wages are one-third to one-half what they are in Mexico. Tellingly, as late as August 2001, when all other bilateral negotiations had been completed, Mexico was still talking with China in an attempt to secure a grace period of at least eight years before it removes duties as high as 1000% on more than 1000 Chinese products. China didn't want to allow more than a three-year grace period, according to Mexico's economy minister.[3] Only on September 13, four days before the WTO Working Party officially approved the accession terms for China's entry, did the two countries finally reach a bilateral agreement.

Economically, China has shown signs of playing both a larger and a more responsible regional and international role. This was notable during the Asian financial crisis. At that time, China contributed $1 billion to the IMF-led rescue for Thailand, the first time it had participated in such a program on anything like that scale. At the same time, Chinese leaders resisted pressure from exporters to devalue the country's currency. A telling moment came during an ASEAN summit meeting in Kuala Lumpur at the end of 1997, when Southeast Asian leaders implored Chinese President Jiang Zemin not to devalue the *yuan*. Jiang's decision not to devalue helped contain the currency contagion and put an end to the cycle of beggar-thy-neighbor devaluations that plagued the region during 1997 and 1998. That commitment to hold firm in the face of pleas by China's beleaguered exporters to devalue marked a key moment in China's emergence as a major regional economic power.

China has also been exercising a more powerful political role as it flexes its growing muscle throughout the region. When the USSR dissolved at the end of 1991, China was just coming out of its post-Tiananmen isolation. In the last 10 years it has had remarkable successes in foreign policy in the region. Despite a powerful US presence in the Pacific, China dominates mainland Asia, where it filled the vacuum left behind by the collapse of the Soviet Union. In 1992, China established diplomatic relations with the Republic of Korea, a longtime enemy. That relationship has gone a long way toward neutralizing the traditional pro-US tilt in South Korea's foreign policy, despite the continuing presence of 37,000 American troops on the peninsula. Seoul's worries about offending China in significant areas reflected in the way it holds back on assistance for North Korean refugees fleeing into China, shows China's power.

Border states such as Burma and Mongolia are effectively within China's orbit. Relations have even stabilized with Vietnam, a country with which China fought a brief but bloody war in the late 1970s that saw 30,000 Chinese soldiers killed. China played a key role in brokering peace in Cambodia. Repeated trips to Southeast Asia by Chinese leaders have helped solidify ties. For China, "it's the best security environment in 150 years," says Robert Ross, a professor at Boston College and an expert on China's foreign policy. "You have a China that can rest content with the status quo" while it concentrates on economic development.[4] Nonetheless, it bears repeating that China is a rising power and that rising powers always occasion disruptions. There are a number of unresolved border and territorial disputes with India and with a number of Southeast Asian nations. Taiwan remains a potential flash point. Moreover, trade tensions between China and countries as disparate as Japan, India and South Korea have been rising as Chinese exports play an increasingly prominent role in trade.

As far as the economic impact of WTO is concerned, the litmus test will be foreign direct investment in China and its regional neighbors. There's widespread agreement that China's accession to the WTO, by regularizing trade and boosting certainty, almost certainly will drive even more foreign investment to China. The granting of Permanent Normal Trading Relations status to China by the US, as required by WTO rules, will put an end to the annual and inevitably controversial one-year renewal of Normal Trade Relations. This uncertainty has kept China from reaching its full potential as an investment destination or an export source. WTO membership means that it will be more difficult for other countries to put curbs on Chinese exports. Foreign direct investment is important because it is correlated with higher overall growth, higher productivity growth and more diversified technology exports.[5]

Despite the lack of investment protection that the WTO promises, China's foreign direct investment already ran at extremely high levels throughout the 1990s. In 1990, China received just $3.4 billion in foreign investment. The figure grew more than tenfold, to $41.7 billion, by 1996. Then it topped $40 billion annually every year from 1996 to 2000. Only a handful of developing countries have ever managed to receive even $10 billion in a single year. Indeed, worldwide, China's inward investment was second only to the United States in the late 1990s, and represented a large percentage of the entire foreign direct investment going to the developing world. Worried Southeast Asian leaders note that a decade ago their region received the overwhelming majority of investment going to East Asia. Now China dominates the investment flows, while Southeast Asia receives just a trickle.

Foreign investment in China should accelerate with WTO accession. Foreign direct investment favors countries with a stable macroeconomic performance and high growth. During most of the 1990s, China had both. Although the disruptions caused by WTO membership could change the equation, the fact that China's leadership has made the courageous decision to join the WTO, despite the risks it entails, shows that China is serious about pursuing difficult reforms. That should put China on a path that's more likely to produce sustainable and stable growth. Barring any political upheaval or protracted economic crisis, foreign direct investment over the next decade is likely to continue to dwarf the investment flows previously directed to a developing country.[6]

How much will direct investment into China increase from the already very high levels that we have seen in the 1990s? At the extremely optimistic end of the spectrum, Fred Hu thinks that China could be sucking in $100 billion annually in direct investment by 2005, nearly as much as the United States does now. That figure would require everything to go right, including the development of a robust domestic market and continued strong export growth. If Hu's figures are correct, the $100 billion would put foreign direct investment at an estimated 6.3% of GDP, compared with 4.5% of a smaller economy in 1998. It's a high figure, but still less as a percentage of GDP than Malaysia received in the early 1990s. Chinese officials think that at least $50 billion a year in foreign investment will flow into China after WTO accession. Though that sounds modest next to Hu's it's still a big slug of money and would ensure that China is among the world's top destinations for foreign investment. Most of the foreign direct investment in the last two decades has gone into export-oriented manufacturing. But as a result of WTO, domestic markets are opening up in areas such as retailing, autos, telecommunications and financial services. The next big foreign investment boom will focus on tapping the Chinese domestic market.[7]

Trade to and from China is booming. Barring a collapse in global trading volumes, the heady growth is expected to continue. In most export areas, the WTO itself won't have a dramatic impact because, as noted previously, most nations already give China WTO-like privileges in the form of Normal Trading Relations. But the combination of China's improved competitiveness in a variety of industries and the reduced uncertainty that will follow WTO entry make for a powerful combination. China will remain, as it has been for some time, one of the most important exporters of labor-intensive, low-end products. But it's increasingly moving up the ladder in its ability to produce ever-more sophisticated goods. For example, China's electronics and other light manufactured goods are increasingly competitive in the world market, thanks in large part to investment from Taiwan and Japan.

A bellwether event for China and much of the developing world will be the elimination of quotas on garments and textiles (the Agreement on Textiles and Clothing) at the end of 2004. Although restrictions will remain on Chinese products exported to the US for an additional four years, the phasing out of quotas will provide another boost for Chinese clothing manufacturers and marks the only major area where China will get significantly more market access as a result of WTO entry. It's in this sector that competitors' fears about an army of Chinese workers producing more goods more cheaply than ever before take shape. World Bank studies estimate that Chinese apparel production will nearly quadruple (up 263.5%) in the decade following accession. The export numbers look even more staggering. China's clothing exports will, according to the Bank, nearly quintuple (up 375%). Its share of the total world clothing export market will surge to more than 47%, compared with 15% in 1997. The good news is that China will be importing many more textiles to make those clothes. Textile imports are expected to nearly quadruple (up 272%).

SOUTHEAST ASIA

It's in Southeast Asia that fears run highest about China's entry. Anecdotally, it seems that these countries have a good deal to worry about. Foreign investment that heads for China rather than Southeast Asia, a flood of cheap Chinese-made goods in labor-intensive industries, coupled with the more sophisticated electronics goods that China is making and the end of textile quotas, all add up to bad news for Southeast Asia. Add in the hangover from the late 1990s financial crisis and the recession in 2001 and it's understandable why the mood in the region's business and political circles is grim. Southeast Asia benefited from the wave of outsourcing that companies from the developed world engaged in during the 1980s and 1990s. But now much of that investment is being wound down in Southeast Asia and transferred to China.

Investment has already dropped sharply from the heady levels of the early and mid-1990s. Yet ASEAN projects that at least another 10% of the foreign investment still destined for the region will be diverted to China.[8] Cheap as labor costs are in Southeast Asia, they are even cheaper in China.

In a study released in late 2000, the ASEAN Secretariat fretted over the future of foreign direct investment in the region. It cautioned that "China commands a distinct advantage over ASEAN" in this regard.

China is a huge and dynamic market. Her economic managers steered the economy ably through the worst of the Asian economic crisis leaving China unscathed. Her political leadership appears to be committed to economic reform. The determined way in which China worked for her accession to the WTO is a demonstration of that commitment. The liberalization of her market is bound to further enhance investor confidence and lower the cost of doing business in the country.

In contrast, ASEAN is a regional grouping with diverse members, cultures and economic systems. The onslaught of the economic crisis unmasked flaws in economic structure and policies which have eroded the confidence of investors.[9]

Wages in China are about 20% less than in the Philippines, and run at only one-third the level of Malaysia and one-quarter that of Thailand, according to ASEAN figures.[10] But cheap workers are only part of the challenge that ASEAN faces. China not only has more workers but more skilled workers. A report by the Japan Bank for International Cooperation notes further problems. China graduates 420,000 engineers a year, while Thailand turns out just 15,000. Even mighty Japan graduates only 160,000. In China, domestic-appliance makers of so-called white goods (appliances such as refrigerators and microwave ovens) have a dominant 70% market share. Chinese manufacturers are going from strength to strength as they build up manufacturing prowess and an increasingly global brand-name presence. Yet in ASEAN, Japanese manufacturers dominate the markets, largely thanks to an extensive network of local factories. Making matters worse, as far as the development of an indigenous manufacturing industry in ASEAN is concerned, even most of the component makers supplying these factories are Japanese. There is alarmingly little local participation in the manufacturing sector.

While ASEAN's electronics production capacities still exceed those of China, thanks to Japanese investment, China is catching up quickly. Ominously, its exports to ASEAN are increasing. Privately, Japanese executives have proposed an alliance with ASEAN to help stem the China challenge, but have expressed their despair that local capabilities are so weak and that the sense of urgency among government and commercial leaders is so low. While ASEAN countries failed to localize imported technology and encourage their domestic industries (especially small- and mid-sized players) to acquire export capabilities, China has made home-grown research-and-development capabilities a priority.[11]

The ASEAN study cautioned that "competition between China and ASEAN countries will be more intense in such labor-intensive products as textiles, clothing, miscellaneous manufactures and electronics". The group went on to warn that China and ASEAN rely on the same export markets — the US, the European Union and Northeast Asia. According to ASEAN data, the US and Japan account for 31.5% of ASEAN's exports and 36.8% of China's exports. "China's entry [will] pose a stiff challenge to countries in ASEAN that rely heavily on clothing and other labor-intensive manufactured exports or rely heavily on electronics exports without sufficient agricultural and mineral resource-based exports to depend on." It noted that Singapore is the biggest loser, in terms of exports, and that it will actually suffer a net loss in exports from China's entry into the WTO.[12]

The report cautions that ASEAN needs to keep pushing ahead with reforms, especially the creation of the ASEAN Free-Trade Area (AFTA) and the ASEAN Investment Area (AIA). However, these goals are unlikely to be achieved. Indeed, the full implementation of AFTA has been pushed back as a result of Malaysian concern that freer trade would hurt its domestic automobile industry. A typical assessment came from the Japan Bank for International Cooperation in a study done in mid-2001: "While China is growing with confidence, ASEAN market unification seems to be stagnant due to inward-looking politics." Given the dominance of Japanese investment in the region, ASEAN needs to keep the confidence of Japanese investors if it's going to have another round of manufacturing-led growth.

Surprisingly, despite the flood of Japanese investment in this area from the mid-1980s to the mid-1990s, the ASEAN Secretariat cautions that the region will have to worry about China as an electrical and electronics exporter. Machinery and electrical appliances made up a measly 2.82% of China's total exports in 1986. In 1998, the figure had leapt to 23.7% of a much larger export base. The ASEAN Secretariat notes that China's share in the US electronics market jumped from 9.5% in 1992 to 21.8% in 1999.[13] During the same period, Singapore's share dropped from 21.8% to 13.4%. Already, China is the world's production center for household electric-appliance manufacturing. According to an unpublished Japanese study, China manufactures 29% of the world's color televisions and washing machines, 32% of its air conditioners and 50% of its photocopiers.

Even in areas where it's not the dominant producer, China made impressive strides during the second half of the 1990s. This was especially true in computers and peripherals, thanks in large part to Taiwanese investment in China. In desktop personal computers, China went from 4% of world production in 1996 to 21% in 2000, at a time when the global industry itself increased dramatically. During the same period, ASEAN's share shrank from 17% to 6%. The situation was similar with hard-disk drives, as China increased its global share from 1% in 1996 to 6% in 2000. ASEAN saw its share during the period drop from 83% to 77%, with its fall nearly mirroring China's gains. With computer keyboards, China's share jumped from 18% to 38% during the 1996–2000 period, while ASEAN's dropped from 57% to 42%.[14]

ASEAN is losing market share in the US to China,

which saw its exports of electronic goods to the US grow two-and-a-half times, to $35 billion, between 1996 and 2000. Comparable ASEAN exports grew 60% during the period, to $40 billion. And, besides finished goods, Chinese exports of components are increasing. "The competition with Japanese parts makers in ASEAN will start," warns the Japan Bank for International Cooperation report.[15]

Certainly, traditional economic theory holds that freer trade allows countries to specialize in what they do best. China's rise in manufacturing will force Southeast Asian countries either to get better or to find some other activity. But what exactly should they focus on if Southeast Asia looks unlikely to be competitive in many areas of manufacturing? So far, South and Southeast Asia's services sector holds out little hope of being internationally competitive, with the notable exception of telephone call centers and IT-related software areas in India and the Philippines. Southeast Asia may find that its comparative advantage lies in agriculture. More sophisticated and higher value-added agricultural products are an area that Southeast Asia clearly needs to focus on.

CHINA AS REGIONAL GROWTH ENGINE

The pronounced tendency to see China's entry into the WTO as a threat may reflect the idea that trade is a zero-sum game. By this way of thinking, if China is a winner, then someone else must be an equivalent loser. Or maybe it's just because China is so big, and because it's increasingly competitive, that its smaller neighbors worry that they'll be run over by this economic juggernaut. The analysis in the preceding section certainly suggests that there is plenty to worry about.

But an alternative, and equally plausible, view contends that the increased amount of foreign direct investment going to China will complement flows to the rest of the region. Yiping Huang, a Hong Kong-based economist at Salomon Smith Barney, believes that the impact of foreign direct investment will outweigh that of trade flows.[16] Huang, who used a statistical analysis of 34 countries from 1985 to 1999, found a positive correlation between the growth of foreign direct investment in China and investment in both Northeast and Southeast Asia. Surprisingly, the correlation was stronger for Southeast Asia than for Northeast Asia.

Huang believes that his research demonstrates the common-sense notion than China and other Asian countries have different comparative strengths and are at different stages of development. As intra-regional trade grows, and as Asia's importance as both a manufacturer and a consumer grows, foreign direct investment into Asia will continue to be strong. He notes that Asia has been losing ground to Latin America since the onset of Asia's financial crisis in 1997, and that Latin America surpassed Asia in foreign direct investment in 1998. (The data extends only through 1999; the effects of the difficulties Latin America experienced in 2001 could change this picture.) Huang says that the increase in Latin America over the past decade has been every bit as compelling as the China story in Asia. Asian policy makers, he argues, are wrong to focus on whether China's share of foreign direct investment in Asia will grow or shrink. Rather, they should focus on Asia's share vis-à-vis the rest of the developing world, especially Latin America.

The question is whether or not Southeast Asia will

have the skilled workers, the enlightened government policies and the favorable environment for business in the years ahead that it had from 1985 to 1999. Those years that Huang studied, after all, coincided with the boom in Southeast Asia. Following the peak of the dollar in February 1985, and the September 1985 Plaza Accord that confirmed a policy of driving the dollar lower and the yen higher, Japanese investors swarmed into Southeast Asia. The yen rose from 260 against the dollar in 1985 to 80 a decade later. As the yen marched higher, low-wage places such as Malaysia, Thailand and Indonesia were natural investment sites for Japanese companies. Many of them brought their Japanese component makers with them, further fueling investment and production in Southeast Asia. At the same time, Japanese investment in China was limited by both numerous restrictions and political uncertainty.

Following that wave of electronics investments, Japanese auto makers set up substantial production facilities, especially in Thailand. They hoped to take advantage of a regional economic market that ASEAN members promised would be introduced. However, political resistance has delayed the introduction of ASEAN's free-trade area (AFTA), with autos subject to continued curbs. Meanwhile, Southeast Asia's weaknesses in education, questions about the consistency of its policies and the quality of its political leadership continue to concern investors.

There may indeed be a new golden age for Southeast Asia on the back of an expanding Chinese economy. But Asia's policy makers will need to step up efforts in everything from basic education to increased corporate reform and a more transparent economic system if they are to take advantage of it.

NORTHEAST ASIA AND GREATER CHINA

Overall, Japan and South Korea stand to benefit handsomely from China's accession to the WTO. Japan is already China's largest export market, surpassing the US. Two-way trade between Korea and China has quintupled since diplomatic relations were established in 1992, to $31 billion in 2000. Significantly, Korea went from a $1 billion deficit to a surplus of nearly $6 billion, as it sold China goods such as petrochemicals and steel that Chinese industry needed. Estimates are that two-way trade between the two countries could total $100 billion annually by 2010. Japanese and Korean exporters of everything from capital goods to electronic components to chemicals to high-quality textiles should continue to see big increases in sales to China, piggybacking off both increased domestic demand and more export-oriented factories in China.

Yet, paradoxically, they are also two countries where trade frictions are likely to be especially pronounced. While makers of many more-sophisticated or capital-intensive goods will prosper, producers of labor-intensive goods in these countries are particularly vulnerable to Chinese exports, for reasons of both geographic and cultural proximity. In other words, Japan and Korea are nearby and their consumers want the sort of specialty products that would be difficult to export to most other countries. That became painfully apparent in 2000, when Seoul imposed high tariffs on Chinese garlic in order to protect its domestic farmers. Korea quickly backed down after China restricted imports of Korean mobile telephones and polyethylene in retaliation. In April 2001, Japan imposed import duties of 266% on imports of shiitake mushrooms from China and duties of 106% for the rushes used to make tatami mats. China retaliated with 100% tariffs on Japanese automobiles, mobile telephones and air conditioners. Other labor-intensive Japanese industries — from chopstick producers to eel and chicken farmers — are looking for protection from Chinese imports. Korea's farmers feel similar pressure.

It's not only farmers who are worried. Throughout the 1990s, China took increasing shares of Korea's market for labor-intensive products in the United States and Europe. More recently, it's been doing the same thing for more sophisticated products. In 1995, Korea accounted for 9% of the US consumer electronics market, while China took 6.9%. But by 2000, Korea's share shrank to 7.8% while China's share rose to 10.5%.

     ð   ð   ð

There's probably no place outside of mainland China that has a greater stake in China's successful WTO accession, and continued economic reform, than Taiwan and Hong Kong. Both the political and economic dimensions of the equations are powerful. As noted, China's renewed interest in acquiring WTO status in the early 1990s in large part reflected a desire not to let Taiwan get in ahead of it or on terms that it was unhappy with. Because of China's claims to sovereignty over Taiwan and the territories it controls, China persuaded the WTO to delay approving Taiwan's accession until China was given the go-ahead to join. Formally, Taiwan doesn't even enter as a country, in accordance with China's long-standing policy of insisting to international organizations that Taiwan cannot enjoy national status. As a result, Taiwan is entering as the Separate

Customs Territory of Taiwan, Penghu, Kinmen and Matsu, abbreviated as Chinese Taipei. Although this is a diplomatic slight, Taiwan will nonetheless enjoy all the rights and have all the obligations of any other WTO member.

China's WTO membership is critical for Taiwan because growing investment by the island's businesses in China has made the economic relationship a critical one for both sides. Yet much of this investment is in legally gray areas because of both Chinese and Taiwanese restrictions. The protection that will go with WTO membership should provide a powerful boost to these growing economic ties. Taiwan's manufacturers spent much of the 1990s making investments in the mainland, following an easing of ties. Costs in Taiwan are rising; besides lower costs and a seemingly unlimited supply of manufacturing workers, the cultural and linguistic identity with Taiwan make the decision to invest in China an easy one. Indeed, in the absence of significant political tension, it would be surprising if economic ties didn't flourish following WTO entry.

Since trade links were forged in the late 1980s, Taiwan's leaders have tried to ensure that the island's economy would not become too dependent on the mainland. Under its "go slow, be patient" policy, Taiwan prohibited investments of more than $50 million in a single project (though businessmen regularly circumvented this ban, by routing investments through Hong Kong or another offshore location) and prohibited investments altogether in some areas. For example, Taiwanese companies in the mainland are prohibited by their government from doing final computer assembly.

Former Taiwan President Lee Teng-hui pushed a "Go South" policy in the mid-1990s, encouraging business to invest in Vietnam as a way of discouraging an over-reliance on China. Taiwan's government-backed Central Trading & Development, an arm of the Kuomintang, set up an entire planned community in Ho Chi Minh City, the business capital of Vietnam. The project includes a massive industrial park and a residential, office and educational community known as Saigon South. Lee also pushed Taiwanese companies to invest in the Philippines, Indonesia and other Southeast Asian countries. Although all this worked well enough, it wasn't enough to keep businesses from going to China.

In just over a decade, and despite official misgivings, Taiwan's investments have been extraordinary. Accurate figures are an impossibility, because legal restrictions mean that many of the investments are routed through places like the British Virgin Islands, but Taiwan officials figure that about $60 billion was invested in the mainland by 80,000 different enterprises from 1990 to 2000. Now, between 200,000 and 300,000 Taiwanese live on the mainland, some with their families. Recently, the island has been smitten with China fever, and moving to Shanghai has become the hip thing for young Taiwanese. The first Taiwanese school in the mainland opened in Guangdong province in 2000. It's a place where Taiwan's educational curriculum can be taught with relatively little interference from mainland authorities. Given the political sensitivities of education, it's a truly extraordinary example of what a budding trade relationship can do for two places that are, technically, still in the midst of a civil war. Taiwanese corporations are helping improve the mainland's technological capabilities. There are several ongoing research projects between Beijing University and Taiwanese companies.

Even with the restrictions, the acceleration of Taiwan's investment in the mainland, especially in the electronics sector, has been stunning. Whole categories of low-end electronics work are moving the bulk of their manufacturing production to the mainland, especially in labor-intensive areas such as manufacturing components for personal computers and other electronic devices. Indeed, thanks in large part to investment from Taiwan, China recently surpassed Taiwan as the world's third-largest producer of information-technology (IT) products. It's expected to pass second-ranked Japan soon, perhaps as early as 2002. Semi-official sources in Taiwan say that IT exports from Taiwan-invested factories in China amounted to $14.6 billion in 2000, about 40% of China's total electronics exports.[17]

Taipei still imposes restrictions on much of the technology manufacturing industry, but business is applying pressure to have these removed. The cost advantage is too high to ignore. Engineers on the mainland cost just one-third of what they do in Taiwan and the differential for production workers is even greater, so companies in this cutthroat business increasingly feel that they have little choice but to move. In the most notable example, Winston Wang, who comes from one of the island's most prominent business families, has set up a semiconductor plant in Shanghai in a partnership with Chinese President Jiang Zemin's son, though Wang says that none of the money is coming from Taiwan. The island's two dominant semiconductor makers, Taiwan Semiconductor Manufac-turing Co. and United Microelectronics Co., cannot afford to flout the ban, but their executives are impatient to see the restrictions lifted.

Taiwan's investors have much to gain from the establishment of a rules-based trading system and the application of more transparency and a more robust legal system. Initially, because of the strained circumstances between the two countries, businessmen had little choice but to act furtively. The mix of a common Chinese culture, the need to conceal actions from Taiwan's authorities and an immature, connections-based economy in China has allowed some of Taiwan's opportunistic businessmen to do well. But this same business culture has presented hurdles for companies wanting to make more capital-intensive investments. To date, Taiwan's business associations have dealt with authorities primarily on a local basis, although they sometimes coordinate relations through Taiwan's Straits Exchange Foundation, the government body that conducts negotiations with the mainland. Increasingly, though, Taiwan's businessmen want better legal protection, particularly in such areas as investment guarantees and bankruptcy codes. WTO status should be a big boost in this area. Additionally, because it's a multilateral organization, it should depoliticize disputes by setting out uniform standards.

In August 2001, a high-level bipartisan panel urged Taiwan to drop its "go slow, be patient" policy in favor of what it called "active opening up, effective management". The panel recommended a broad range of changes to loosen restrictions on travel, trade and investment. The new proposals make it likely that even companies in sophisticated industries such as semiconductors will soon be able to invest legally in the mainland. As part of this package, the government in Taipei also agreed to push for the rapid establishment of direct transportation and communication links. As it is now, Taiwan's business people must make a costly and time-consuming detour, usually through Hong Kong, to get to the mainland. Increasingly, their operations are in Fuzhou or in or around Shanghai, locations that are little more than an hour away by air across the Taiwan Strait. But the existing arrangements force them to spend the better part of a day traveling, usually via Hong Kong. These negotiations are not part of WTO arrangements, for transportation links are subject only to bilateral negotiations, but WTO membership will add to the momentum to establish direct transportation links.

For the most part, Beijing has kept politics and economics on two separate tracks. It has worked assiduously to deny Taiwan political legitimacy, while fostering economic ties. But occasionally it uses businesses to make a political point. In 2000, local authorities in China investigated Chi Mei Industry. The company's Taiwanese owner is a prominent supporter of Taiwan's President Chen Shui-bian, who had been elected earlier that year, despite Beijing's opposition. They held up needed imports and checked the company for alleged business violations, while making it clear that the probe was meant as political retaliation. Other companies with ties to Chen say that they, too, have been subject to harassment.

When it comes to specific industries, China's accession will pose some challenges for Taiwan. Agriculture will be the industry that suffers the most. Chinese farmers can produce green vegetables, mushrooms and the like far more cheaply than farmers in Taiwan. Authorities worry that farmers in the Taipei area will be especially vulnerable. As in every country, this will present formidable political problems. It will be interesting to see if Taiwan's authorities surrender to the temptation to use phytosanitary standards, by imposing difficult standards on imported food, to stem what could be a formidable export of fresh food, especially after direct air and shipping links are established. Financial flows are another problem area. Given its level of economic development and the size of its foreign-exchange reserves, Taiwan still maintains extensive capital controls. In large part, the caution reflects concern that Chinese capital could disrupt the island's economy by, for example, driving up stock prices and then withdrawing the funds precipitously. Yet the bipartisan panel that recommended direct transportation links in its August 2001 report also called for direct financial transfers across the Taiwan Strait.

&ã   &ã   &ã

In the short run, China's WTO entry will almost certainly benefit the former British colony of Hong Kong. Since 1997, Hong Kong has been a Special Administrative Region of China, accelerating a process of economic integration that has been under way since economic reforms on the mainland began in 1978. Hong Kong's port and airport are a key entrepot for China's massive export machine. Hong Kong's growth rises and falls in time with the rhythm of the Chinese economy. If China booms after WTO accession, then Hong Kong should benefit.

Still, WTO will be a testing time for the city of seven million people. Hong Kong's boosters say that the mainland's continued economic growth will power a new wave of growth for the enclave. The optimists argue that the territory's strong institutional underpinnings (rule of law and freedom of the press) coupled with the bedrock of professional services companies (lawyers, accountants, investment bankers and the like) and the supply-chain management sophistication of many of the city's companies give Hong Kong a strong position. It has some of the world's best infrastructure, including a striking airport and the world's busiest port. An aggressive telecommunications deregulation policy during the 1990s has ensured that its data and telecommunications service is both reliable and inexpensive. The city kicked off a campaign in mid-2001 to bill itself as "Asia's World City", a regional services hub that can allow companies to take advantage of excellent infrastructure and a pro-business, can-do spirit.

Hong Kong already qualifies as one of the most services-oriented economies in the world, with services accounting for 85% of its GDP. While Singapore has consciously tried to hold onto its manufacturing base, Hong Kong bowed to market forces and let its manufacturing jobs move across the border after China opened its economy in 1978. Despite fears that the economy would hollow out, it has thrived, and Hong Kong companies now control factories employing an estimated six million people in neighboring Guangdong province. Its lawyers and investment bankers do a handsome business helping companies list on the stock market — Hong Kong's stock market is increasingly driven by mainland investments — and sealing deals for everything from infrastructure projects to joint-venture factories on the mainland. In many ways, the transition that Hong Kong has undergone since 1978 is a textbook example of economic flexibility and comparative advantage.

If all goes well, Hong Kong could end up as the commercial center of a vast metropolitan region. Add in the cities of Guangzhou, Dongguan and Shenzhen on the rich eastern edge of the Pearl River delta and the metropolitan population totals more than 26 million people. Shenzhen, the roaring border town with four million people, has a per capita income of $6200, while the income of Guangzhou, the provincial capital, is almost $3800 per head. Those income figures put them ahead of Shanghai ($3300) and Beijing ($2800) and make these delta cities China's richest. Already, approximately one in every five households in Shenzhen owns a car and seven out of ten families own their own homes or apartments. If Hong Kong can find a way to integrate itself more closely with China's richest consumer market, it should do well. So far, though, Hong Kong companies have had only limited success in investing in the mainland. Notably, Hong Kong's vaunted property developers have fared poorly in the mainland despite their hometown might. For both economic and political reasons, Hong Kong largely has preferred to keep its distance from neighboring Guangdong.

The danger, then, is that the city becomes irrelevant to much of what happens in China. From the birth of Communist China until the 1990s, Hong Kong had an effective monopoly on the China trade. Even after economic reforms on the mainland began in 1978, Hong Kong was *the* place from which to do China business. Executives and managers traveled frequently to Shanghai or Beijing, but relatively few foreign businesses actually installed their executives there. As China is opening up, all that is changing. Hong Kong is far more expensive than the mainland for most goods and services. There are more qualified English-speaking staff in Beijing and Shanghai than in Hong Kong. Hong Kong has been extremely cautious about letting in mainland residents, for fear of adding to the woes of a city that has suffered from falling property values, grinding deflation and rising joblessness in the wake of the Asian financial crisis of the late 1990s. Although the border crossing that connects Hong Kong with the city of Shenzhen is one of the world's busiest, Hong Kong officials have proven reluctant to extend border opening hours for fear of putting further deflationary pressure on property and retail prices in Hong Kong. Yet the fear of bowing to market forces and embracing closer economic integration with the mainland may damage Hong Kong's long-term economic prospects.

The hope in Hong Kong is that the China pie will grow so much that Hong Kong will prosper even as its share of the pie shrinks. For the next five to 10 years, that strategy will almost certainly work. But looking a decade or more out, Hong Kong's position looks less secure. If recently launched educational reforms have the intended effect of producing a more flexible, creative and skilled workforce, Hong Kong will have a fighting chance at keeping its vaunted position as China's international window over a longer time period. But the rise of an increasingly skilled Chinese workforce, as well as direct transportation links with Taiwan, means that Hong Kong will have to fight to keep its privileged place. For example, direct Taiwan–China flights could severely dent profits at Hong Kong's unofficial flag carrier, Cathay Pacific, whose most profitable route is that between Hong Kong and Taipei. Paradoxically, Hong Kong is in the uncomfortable position of needing China to develop rapidly enough that the city's expensive cadre of highly skilled professionals and its impressive port and airport facilities are kept busy

— but not so quickly that business forsakes Hong Kong for Shanghai, Beijing or even Guangzhou.

THE GREATER MEKONG SUBREGION: A CASE STUDY IN COOPERATIVE EFFORTS

One potential area for cooperation between China and its neighbors is in the Greater Mekong subregion, which includes the southern Chinese province of Yunnan. China has been intensively involved in this effort, making it, by Chinese standards, a major regional initiative. Its partners read China's intensive involvement as evidence that China wants to open up and to play a more positive role in building regional stability. Given Yunnan's poverty, the project is also a way to encourage development in one of China's less prosperous regions and fits in with a national policy to develop China's inland regions. Although the project has the potential to increase regional trade cooperation, it also shows the difficulties inherent in implementing a scheme that appears to make perfect sense on paper. The Mekong project helps illustrate the real-world challenges involved in China acting as a regional political leader and catalyst for growth, particularly in a diverse and largely impoverished region.

In 1992, the six countries that share the mighty Mekong River launched a program to increase regional cooperation. (The six countries are Burma, Cambodia, Laos, Thailand, Vietnam and China — specifically, Yunnan province.) The idea was simple: to promote economic links and thus to increase living standards and social well-being. Although the six countries are varied in their respective economic development and political orientation, the idea of investing in areas like transportation, energy resources and telecommunications that would benefit all had an obvious appeal. In most of the region, infrastructure is lacking. Much of the area's limited trade is clandestine. With the exception of Thailand, all of these are, to a greater or lesser degree, planned economies. More infrastructure should not only create more economic opportunities but also build better political and economic relations in a region that has suffered repeated conflicts over the past half-century. The increase in economic activity, in turn, should build up basic organizations such as chambers of commerce and create the legal framework for more private-sector activity.

There are few road, rail or air links, making interregional trade difficult. There are more than six round-trip flights a day between Hong Kong and Bangkok that cross the Mekong region. But there are few flights between these major cities and the region, and few within the region. For example, there are no flights between the Cambodian capital, Phnom Penh, and Burma's capital, Rangoon. Flights have been increasing between Thailand and Yunnan, but China could do more. It has adopted policies to protect Yunnan's provincial airline against competition from Thai Airways, despite the overall positive economic impact that a more open transport market would have on the province.

New investments in basic infrastructure, along with policies allowing goods and services to flow more freely across the region's borders, should expand economic activity, especially in border areas, which are typically among the poorest areas of these countries. The development program is also intended to improve health and education services for ethnic minorities, who are typically among the poorest people in many of these countries. Region-wide transmission networks can cut the cost of providing telecommunications services and electricity. Finally, the program wants to tackle common regional environmental problems, problems that hurt the poor disproportionately. Transportation improvements are particularly important. Halving transportation costs typically results in almost a doubling of trade.[18]

Two major regional infrastructure projects are under way. Construction has begun on a highway to connect Phnom Penh with Ho Chi Minh City, Vietnam's southern commercial capital. Another, the East-West Corridor project, will link Burma, Laos, Thailand and Vietnam. This will provide ocean port access, through Vietnam, for Laos, Cambodia and parts of Thailand's interior. Yet, a decade after the cooperation program began, the two highway projects, out of 10 financed with Asian Development Bank support, are the only ones that cross national borders. (The other projects are national ones, although they should have positive regional spillover effects.) With the cross-border projects, delays resulted because of difficulties in reaching agreement on the cross-border movement of goods and people.

Two other regional infrastructure projects are high priority. The North-South Corridor consists of an improved road link between Kunming, Yunnan's capital, and the northern Thai city of Chiang Rai. Another project will improve road, rail and river links between Kunming and the Vietnamese capital of Hanoi and the nearby port of Haiphong. Separately, an agreement for Mekong navigation will, for the first time, regulate traffic on the river. Shipping costs should be reduced as a result of establishing clear rules. Yunnan has already joined with Burma, Laos and

Thailand to sign a navigation pact that will permit commercial use of the river on an internationally regulated basis. Yunnan, in particular, has benefited from the cross-border linkages. It's mostly Chinese boats that ply the Mekong between Jinghong and Chiang Rai, carrying Chinese fruits for export to neighboring markets. After WTO accession there should be more exports of farm products from these countries into China.

Thanks to the new attention on the Mekong, trade and investment within the region has grown. Thailand's exports to Cambodia, Laos and Burma grew at a compound annual rate of 44% from 1992 to 1999. Yet, even at the end of the period, those countries accounted for only 3% of Thailand's exports, up from 0.5% in 1992. The US, by contrast, takes about one-fifth of Thailand's annual exports.[19] ASEAN countries have played an important role in regional investment. ASEAN foreign direct investment into the region during the period 1995–98 totaled $6 billion. That exceeded the $4.8 billion Japan invested during the period and the $2.7 billion that Europe and the US each invested. Although the amounts are small compared to what larger countries in the region receive, they represent significant amounts of money in these tiny economies. These investments and the surge in Thai exports show that cultivating regional ties can stoke growth. If these ties grow, they may also, over time, help more-developed ASEAN countries balance the dependence on large export markets in the US and Europe. But the amounts are so small that, for now, this is little more than fantasy. Even with significant attention from international institutions such as the Asian Development Bank, development is, for the most part, an achingly slow process.

The region's poverty also works against economic development. There's little interest in locating export-oriented factories far from good transportation links — one reason that foreign direct investment has largely bypassed the region. Multinationals have little interest in the region's consumers, especially in small, landlocked countries like Laos, where the population is not only poor but small, and more than half of the country's government budget comes from foreign aid. By any measure, the region qualifies as poor. Per capita income in the area is a paltry $1 a day. Even in relatively wealthy Thailand, about 13% of the population, or nearly 10 million people, are poor, especially in the northeastern part of the country bordering on Laos. About 4.4 million of Yunnan's 41 million people are classified as poor, with an annual per capita income of less than $77, or less than 20 cents a day.

The regional financial turmoil that began in 1997 and set off economic reverberations that are still being felt, hobbled the rapid development of the Mekong region. Hopes of becoming the next East Asian dynamos disappeared along with the money that was pulled out of the region by nervous foreign lenders. "International investors are showing little interest in the [Mekong region] countries which are seen as high risk environments," concluded the Asian Development Bank analysis of the project, noting that only one of more than a dozen investment funds set up during the 1990s to focus on Vietnam still operates.[20]

What development there has been comes at a high cost. Environmental problems remain severe, as the depressing catalogue of woes in the Asian Development Bank report on the region makes clear. Pressing environmental issues include deforestation, soil erosion, water pollution, flooding, overfishing, overuse of pesticides, illegal trade in wildlife and sedimentation of irrigation reservoirs. Environmental damage must be closely monitored as development proceeds. That would be important anywhere, but it's especially so in the Mekong region, where the wise use of the region's wealth of natural resources represents its best hope of sustained economic development. There are also human health costs. Increasing social and work mobility has tremendous benefits, but it's also associated with the spread of HIV/AIDS. The Mekong project's backers promise that they will try to control the transmission of such diseases, especially among high-risk mobile people such as truck drivers, sailors, sex workers and construction workers. But experience in other developing countries gives little hope that the effort will be successful. Even the much-vaunted transportation links have a downside: the roads make it easier for the region's illegal loggers and miners to export their bounty.

The 10 years since the Mekong regional project began is a short time in economic development. Some work has been done, though it would be fair to say that there has been more talk than action. The rapid mobilization of resources that many East Asian countries marshaled during their high-growth periods is a reminder of what can be done in a decade. Even allowing for the inevitable difficulties of negotiations that involve a number of states, the relative lack of progress that has been achieved is a sobering reminder of the difficulty of development. It is one thing to talk about the benefits of trade and globalization, another to realize those benefits in practice. China's role bears watching. Although it has been largely constructive to date, projects such as a proposal to build two dams in Yunnan could cause tensions. Critics of the dams contend that the projects could cause ecological disruption downstream.[21]

        🐌   🐌   🐌

As a rising economic and political power, China will inevitably cause some disruptions in established regional patterns. This will be a threat to some countries and many companies. But, to the extent that it acts to spur changes at both the level of individual companies as well as on the broader national and regional levels, China's accession to the WTO and the resumption of its place as a regional economic power will bring enormous benefits. The WTO accession is the latest and loudest warning bell signaling China's arrival. How its neighbors respond to this warning will determine whether or not they prosper in a new order, one which in Asia will increasingly revolve around China.

---

1   *South China Morning Post*, August 20, 2001. Jake Lloyd-Smith, "Goh Tackles China Challenge."

2   ING Barings *Economics Update*, "What if China is the world's lowest-cost producer of everything?" Tim Condon, August 8, 2001 (mimeo).

3   Geri Smith, "Is the Magic Fading?", *BusinessWeek*, August 6, 2001; Andrea Mandel-Campbell, "Mexico Seeks Deal on China Joining WTO", *Financial Times*, August 14, 2001.

4   Robert Ross's remarks are from an Asia Society meeting in Hong Kong, April 6, 2001.

5   The World Bank's *China 2020: China Engaged*, Washington, D.C., The World Bank, 1997, has a good discussion of China's foreign direct investment and its consequences (pp. 20–23). Although the data dates from the mid-1990s, the basic analysis is even truer than when the book

was published. In 1995, China received 40% of all foreign direct investment in the developing world and 10% of cross-border commercial debt flows. In 1995, foreign direct investment accounted for 25% of total domestic investment, 13% of industrial output, 31% of exports, 11% of tax revenues and 16 million jobs.

[6] One complicating factor in these numbers is that some of the "foreign" investment in China is simply Chinese capital sent back to the country from abroad in the guise of foreign investment in order to qualify for favorable tax and other incentives. These incentives will end with WTO entry, so presumably there will be less incentive to engage in this sort of round-tripping, as the practice is known. If so, that would push down the reported foreign investment numbers. However, what matters to the rest of the developing world is if capital is being diverted from, for example, Southeast Asia or Latin America to China. That remains a real concern. For a more sanguine view, see Rahul Jacob, "Undue Pessimism Clouds South-east Asia Outlook", *Financial Times*, August 14, 2001.

[7] For an alternative view, one that contends foreign investment is unlikely to grow much from the current levels, see Jiang Xiaojuan, "Foreign Investment After China's WTO Accession: Trend and Salient Features", in Ippei Yamazawa and Ken-ichi Imai (eds.), *China Enters WTO: Pursuing Symbiosis with the Global Economy,* Tokyo, Japan External Trade Organization, 2001. Jiang argues that the already high level of foreign investment coupled with stiff competition from domestic and foreign producers, as well as the gradual opening of markets under WTO agreements, means that foreign investment is unlikely to grow more than 5% annually.

[8] ASEAN's older members include Singapore, Thailand, Malaysia, Indonesia, Philippines and Brunei. In the late 1990s, Burma, Cambodia, Vietnam and Laos joined.

[9] ASEAN Secretariat, *China's Membership in the World Trade Organization and Its Implications for ASEAN*, November 2000, p, 24 (mimeo).

[10] *Ibid.,* Table 4, p. 12.

[11] Japan Bank for International Cooperation, *A View of the Asia Economy and Industry — The Development of the China Economy and the Industry vs. ASEAN*, June 2001, pp. 6–7 (mimeo). The Japanese frustration reflects a feeling that, despite the hand-wringing, ASEAN has shown little concrete action.

[12] *China's Membership in the World Trade Organization and Its Implications for ASEAN, op.cit.*, p. 4.

[13] *Ibid.*, p. 16.

14 All numbers are from *A View of the Asia Economy and Industry, op.cit.,* Attachment 1, citing Fuji Chimera Research Institute Inc. and World Wide Electronics, 2000.

15 *Ibid.,* p. 2.

16 Yiping Huang, "WTO Entry: China's Boon, Asia's Bane?", in Salomon Smith Barney, *Asian Economics: Outlook and Strategy,* June 2001, pp. 11–29 (mimeo).

17 "Made in China", *Asiaweek,* July 27 – August 3, 2001.

18 *Eliminating World Poverty: Making Globalisation Work for the Poor, White Paper on International Development, Presented to Parliament by the Secretary of State for International Development,* London, The Stationery Office, 2000, p. 73.

19 Asian Development Bank, *The Greater Mekong Subregion Economic Cooperation Program,* October 2000, p. 4 (mimeo).

20 *Ibid.,* p. 3.

21 Associated Press, "Dam wall rises over Mekong neighbours' objections", *South China Morning Post,* October 3, 2001.

CHAPTER 5

China's Challenge: Accelerating Domestic Reforms

There is an extraordinary irony in the worry with which so much of the rest of the world regards China's entry into the WTO: China's officials and companies are every bit as afraid of what WTO membership will mean for them. While its regional competitors fear its unstoppable rise, China's homegrown enterprises worry about the thundering herd of savvy, well-financed, technologically sophisticated foreign companies that they believe will invade China after WTO accession. Officials fret that the withering competition and the lay-offs that will follow will mean even more social unrest in a country that already has to deal with tens of thousands of demonstrations a year.

They are right to worry. Important props for state domination of the economy will be eliminated. Restrictions on retailing and distribution will be eased, removing a significant competitive barrier. For example, foreign retailers such as Wal-Mart will be able to set up 100%-owned operations and all barriers on distribution by foreign players will be phased out over three years. At present, foreign retailers can only open 50%-owned joint ventures with central-government approval, and are limited to distributing goods made in China. Also, foreign retailers must use a Chinese company for distribution. In telecommunications, foreign players will be able to buy up to 50% of a carrier — up from zero now. In autos, a slew of regulations will be loosened. The same is true in sectors from finance to farming. (Many of the details of these changes are in the Appendices at the end of the book.) The opportunities that WTO-mandated liberalization will open up for foreign companies are extraordinary. The centuries-old vision of tapping China's vast market may finally come to fruition, at least for those companies that have the skills to take advantage of this opening. The important point is that foreigners will have the right to compete in China according to clearly defined rules.

Difficult as these challenges may be for many Chinese enterprises, the decision by President Jiang Zemin and Premier Zhu Rongji to join the WTO reflects a belief that domestic reform needs the external pressure of WTO entry. As far as China's leaders are concerned, the most important reason for China to join the organization is to ensure that domestic reforms continue. It's very much in China's own domestic interest to see that implementation of WTO standards succeeds. Although that may seem counter-intuitive, because the WTO's main role is to ensure that trade develops according to internationally accepted rules, China hopes that the introduction of a rules-based system will anchor its own domestic reforms.

China's leaders know that they need to set rules of the game for their economy. Otherwise, economic growth will be hostage to local protectionism, rampant corruption, and unclear and opaque policies. And it's because China's leaders know that adopting the WTO is in their own interest that

China's entry is likely to succeed both in accelerating China's economic transformation and in strengthening the trade organization. While it would be a mistake to downplay the formidable difficulties China will have in implementing WTO procedures and commitments, critics' fears that its commitment to reform is shallow and that it won't seriously attempt to implement WTO rules miss this pivotal point: China's leaders have made a risky and courageous choice to use accession to the WTO as a way of ensuring that the domestic reform process continues at a time when it otherwise could be losing momentum.

It might seem odd that China's economy would need a boost when it rode out the Asian crisis of the late 1990s with little apparent distress and continues to record an impressive 7%-plus annual growth rate, even during the 2001 downturn that hammered other Asian economies. Yet China faces some daunting challenges. Its banking sector is hobbled by bad debts and shows few signs of moving to more market-oriented credit policies. There are massive unfunded liabilities in the pension system. Its industrial sector is awash in capacity of everything from televisions to steel to refrigerators. The government is understandably reluctant to pay the price of the social upheavals that could ensue if non-performing companies were put out of business too quickly, so the corporate restructuring process will probably stretch on for the better part of a decade.

The situation is every bit as grim for most of the country's 400 million peasants. China's agricultural output is dominated by low productivity in commodity products such as rice, wheat and cotton. It has just begun to move away from the long-cherished notion of agricultural self-sufficiency. It has started to import a small amount of rice under a cumbersome quota system. But China needs to push aggressively into the production of higher value-added farm products. Reforms to guarantee longer lease periods and encourage landholding consolidation are needed. Above all, it must ensure that it doesn't repeat the mistakes of its Northeast Asian neighbors, South Korea and Japan, which squandered vast resources in protecting an inefficient agricultural sector.

Although the Chinese economy has had an extraordinary run since reforms began in 1978, sustained high growth will need continued reform and liberalization. Compliance with WTO requirements gives shape to a reform process that has been experimental and has had no clear goal. Deng Xiaoping remarked that economic reform should proceed cautiously, and that the country should "cross the river by feeling the stones". Jiang Zemin and Zhu Rongji have proceeded in this same vein. The country's stated goal is to build a "socialist market economy", though it's not clear just what such an economy entails. Russia and the Eastern European countries have stated explicitly that they want to build free-market economies. China's leaders have always shied away from any sort of explicit commitment about their economic goals. They haven't had to, partly because most people benefited in the initial decades of reforms. But it's now getting to a point where the choices become much more painful to many more people, and resistance to fundamental reform is stiffening among those with the most to lose. The discipline of WTO rules should underpin further reforms.

Much of the post-1978 growth reflected one-time events, such as the freeing up of the agricultural sector to allow private production and the initial investment ebullience that accompanied the lifting of controls in a variety of areas. The catch-up effect, which saw a surge of activity among farmers and entrepreneurs who were freed from state planning, fueled an extraordinary boom in investment — and saw a handsome pay-off in increased output. During the 1990s, China made the transition from a scarcity economy, where almost everything was in short supply, to a surplus economy. Now, competition among companies is biting. On top of that, China's decision not to devalue its currency in the wake of the East Asian financial crisis has put continuing pressure on its exporters. Chinese exporters have had to compete with regional rivals in countries where currencies have depreciated 20% or more since 1997. The 25 million workers who have lost their jobs at state-owned enterprises since 1998 have also acted to dampen consumption. Other workers, worried about losing their jobs, naturally have tended to spend less and save more. But the biggest problem is excess capacity. One of the least-understood developments of the past decade has been China's transformation from a scarcity economy to a glut economy; from one where virtually everything was in scarce supply to one where there is excess capacity in most manufactured and agricultural products.

Indeed, since 1997, Chinese officials have been forced to use heavy government spending to offset deflation. They've even tried setting minimum prices, encouraged cartels and coordinated production shutdowns in an effort to boost prices of goods such as televisions. Besides heavy fiscal spending, China has resorted to the novel idea of what could be called "holiday economics". Since 1999, authorities have given the entire country a week-long vacation at least twice a year in an attempt to stimulate tourism and consumption. It's a big change from the dreary days of state socialism. Just as important, it actually seems to be having some effect in boosting spending.

Although China's policy responses show a laudable creativity, only sweeping changes in the legal and administrative system can pave the way for sustained economic growth. Bear in mind that it's historically unprecedented for a one-party state with a planned economy to evolve smoothly into a market economy. The huge size of the Chinese government and the considerable power wielded by local authorities make market-oriented reform even more difficult. The legal system is primitive and acts more as a way to transmit state directives than to dispense justice in an impartial fashion.

The WTO will help to erode many of these barriers to reform. As part of the price of WTO entry, China promised a great deal of market access, although it gained very little additional access from foreign trading partners in return. Chinese leaders conceded so much because they know that an external agent such as the WTO will lock reforms into place in a way that internal directives never could. This choice means surrendering a degree of national sovereignty and forcing China's government to adhere to a new set of international norms. Aggrieved foreign businesses will be able to appeal to a higher authority when faced with local protectionism or official opacity.

There's an added benefit to WTO membership that may prove the most important of all, and that's the role it will play in forcing China to build more independent institutions, something that China needs to do if it's to ensure sustained economic growth. One of the most important lessons of the Asian financial crisis is that strong institutions — central banks, regulators and courts — are critical to ensuring survival when a financial typhoon hits. Although Singapore and Hong Kong are among the world's most open economies, they came through Asia's financial crisis in far better shape than South Korea, Indonesia and Thailand. Authorities there couldn't predict the crisis — virtually no one did — but they could and did ensure that their financial institutions were prepared to withstand the sort of storm that only hits once or twice in a century. As China becomes more integrated with the world economy, even its vast continental economy will be buffeted by passing economic storms. Better regulators and better institutions will be needed to prevent disaster when economic storms hit, whether they come from inside the country (such as bank runs) or outside.

The most obvious immediate impact of WTO entry will be continued heavy flows of foreign direct investment. As noted, China's annual average of $40 billion in recent years dwarfs that of other developing countries and is second only to the United States. Yet foreign investment looks like it has nowhere to go but up. Foreign direct investment is one of the most important factors in the continued transformation of the Chinese economy. Foreign capital typically invests in more sophisticated and more profitable areas of the economy and is associated with new technologies and new work and managerial skills. Given the huge size of China's domestic economy, there is a debate about the actual impact of foreign direct investment. Analysts who downplay the importance point out that trade is equivalent to less than one-quarter of the economy (23%

in 2000). But foreign investment is what builds the new factories that are making China a global exporting powerhouse, money that is bringing new technologies and transforming China into an increasingly important global exporting power. Foreign-invested operations now account for about half of China's exports. Increasingly, foreign direct investment is also aimed at the domestic market. It's this investment that is building the automobile plants and food-processing factories that represent the future for China's economy. And it's the foreign-invested sector which employs the best and brightest — and most highly paid — of China's workers.

WTO status reduces the risk premium that potential foreign investors attach to China by providing more policy certainty. More certainty and a lower risk premium improve the risk-reward ratio. That means foreign investors won't demand as high a return to offset the risk of investing. Warwick McKibbin, head of the economics department at the Australian National University, calculates that a one percentage point drop in foreign investors' risk premium, in conjunction with the tariff reductions and other liberalizations mandated as part of the WTO agreement, would see China's economy grow about 1% more annually than it would otherwise. He calculates that the cumulative effect of this would be an economy that, in the sixth year following WTO accession, is 5% larger than it would be without WTO accession. Conventional models, which look only at the impact of tariff reform, predict a 3% increase, which means roughly $30–$50 billion in additional annual output at the end of five years.[1]

LEGAL AND ADMINISTRATIVE REFORMS

Accession to the WTO will present the toughest test that China's weak legal system has ever faced. As part of the price of WTO entry, China has promised to live up to international standards of transparency, accountability and fairness. No one should be sanguine about China's ability to cope with the legal and administrative reforms that it has promised as part of the WTO accession agreement. Yet the ability to implement these changes will be essential to determining the success of this accession. If it can implement the necessary improvements, they should have a tremendous spillover effect on China's overall legal system as well as on continued economic reform.

Genuine economic development cannot occur without a strong legal system. World Bank data shows that countries with good legal institutions are richer, more literate and have dramatically lower rates of infant mortality. World Bank President James Wolfensohn emphasizes that governments should recognize that "an effective legal and judicial system is not a luxury, but a central component of a well-functioning state and an essential ingredient in long-term development". The decision to build a stronger legal system isn't just a technical issue. It is, as Wolfensohn noted, a profoundly political one.[2] And here it's hard to be optimistic about China. Officials talk too often of rule *by* law. Only the most enlightened talk of the rule *of* law, a system that in the courtroom puts a citizen on equal footing with the government.

The implications for China's system of administering laws — in effect, for governing — may be the most important part of the WTO arrangements. Yet they merit a scant two pages in the protocol for China's entry into the organization. The central promise: China promises to apply and administer its laws in a "uniform, impartial and reasonable" manner and it promises a good deal of transparency in how it makes and implements its regulations.

Uniform laws mean that provincial and municipal officials cannot pass local laws that are inconsistent with WTO obligations. Every bit as important, it means that they cannot issue regulations that are at odds with WTO norms. In a country where implementing regulations are often more important than the broadly drawn laws that provide a framework, this promise of uniformity is essential. *Impartial* enforcement of laws marks another cornerstone of the new order. Arbitrary decisions that obviously favor a particular party will be illegal. *Reasonable* laws and regulations should also undercut the tendency to adopt measures that aren't in keeping with basic principles of fairness.

Transparency — the promise, as part of WTO accession, to publish and make readily available all laws, regulations and other measures relating to trade and foreign exchange — marks another momentous step forward for China. There is nothing in the often arbitrary, and almost always secretive, centuries-old style of elite administrative government that will prepare China's officials for this sort of sunshine regulation. What makes the WTO agreement even more powerful is China's promise that all relevant laws and regulations are, in principle, to be released for public comment before they take effect. Only in emergency situations can laws and regulations be announced at the time they are enforced. In no case can laws be imposed retroactively.

China has also pledged that it will establish an official

journal to publicize all trade-related laws, regulations and other measures. Proposed laws and regulations will be published in this journal and a reasonable period of time will be allowed for public comment in the case of most changes. There are limited exceptions regarding national security, foreign-exchange rates, monetary policy and other measures that would impede law enforcement, but the overall tenor of the promise is clear: China will give the world notice of proposed changes to its trade regime and take interested parties' comments into account.

China also has established an enquiry point where any person or company can obtain any, or even all, of China's trade-related laws and regulations. There is a 30-day deadline for replies to requests for information. In exceptional cases, the government may take up to 45 days, but only with a notice of the delay and an explanation of the reason for the delay. The replies must be complete. They will represent the authoritative view of the Chinese government on the subject, so they can be used as support in any subsequent legal proceeding. It's hard to overstate the importance of such a body in a country with a long tradition of opaque, and sometimes inconsistent and seemingly arbitrary, administrative rulings.

Judicial Review: China will set up procedures, perhaps in the form of tribunals, for the timely review of all administrative actions involving trade-related issues. It promises that these tribunals will be impartial and that they will be independent of the agency involved in the case. It will also set up a system to allow for appealing against the decisions of the body. Although the initial appeal may be to an administrative body, all cases will have the right of appeal to a judicial body.

Non-discrimination: China promises that, except for some exceptional areas, it won't discriminate against foreign companies. The principles here are both very broad and very explicit. Foreigners cannot be discriminated *against*. But discrimination *in favor of* Chinese companies will also be prohibited. This principle of non-discrimination is a prerequisite to ensure that the WTO ideal of a level playing field for all will have a good chance of being realized. In practical terms, this means that transportation or electricity subsidies to troubled state-owned enterprises will be prohibited. As part of the accession procedure, China had to detail the subsidies that it provided and promise to eliminate many of them. Subsidies to state-owned industries, which totaled $900 million in 1998, were eliminated as of year-end 2000, as part of the accession agreement.

All in all, the scope of what China vows to do is breathtaking. As far as many Chinese are concerned, and certainly as far as the Chinese government is concerned, the most immediate affect of WTO accession won't be economic. It will be bureaucratic. Although almost a century has elapsed since the collapse of the Qing dynasty, the style of governance hasn't changed a great deal. Laws and regulations are still handed down from on high. And local officials often use the large latitude they enjoy to impose a variety of regulations and fees. This is a fact of everyday Chinese life that affects Chinese businesses and ordinary citizens even more than it affects foreign businesses. It will be illuminating to see how China's increasingly rights-conscious population uses some of the openings that WTO membership promises.

Not surprisingly, there is much that remains uncertain. The mechanisms and procedures to govern this new world haven't yet been set out. What will judicial review consist of? Will there be separate and free-standing courts? Or will there be some sort of arbitration panel? The standards of what is impartial — or what is reasonable — haven't yet been determined. They are, of course, very much open to interpretation. With local protectionism rampant and provinces and municipalities still in the earliest stages of implementing the revisions, it will be a long road ahead. Fortunately, China isn't completely on its own in trying to turn these laudable principles into reality. For a start, the World Bank and the US-government-funded Asia Foundation will train legal drafters (the people who actually write legislation) in all of China's 27 provinces and four self-governing municipalities.

On a more fundamental level, China has yet to enact an administrative law, a comprehensive piece of legislation governing what the powers of the various parts of the government are. An administrative law is a core piece of legislation because it codifies the rights and responsibilities of different parts of the government. As part of an extremely ambitious timetable, China aims to have a draft of an administrative procedure law ready for presentation to the National People's Congress at the end of 2003. The new law will define the coercive powers of the government and specify which bodies can exercise them. It also will define what parts of government have the right to impose taxes. The law will also detail what parts of government have licensing powers and define those powers. And it will specify how an incorporated business can make a complaint against the government.

Interestingly, the central government has a good deal to gain from this exercise. These initiatives should allow central authorities to recapture some of the ground they lost to the provinces during the heady days of economic reform in the 1980s and 1990s. In the area of taxes, for example, in 2000 the entire Chinese government collected only about 14.2% of GDP in tax revenue, an extraordinarily low level by international standards. Of this, the central government's share was 58%.[3] Authorities have made increased tax collections an increasingly important priority in recent years. They have been trying to cut down on the number of locally collected fees in favor of increased taxes in order to give the central government greater control over revenues. An administrative procedures law, and the WTO's requirements for legal consistency and fairness, could help break up local fiefdoms and the protectionism that goes with them.

There's a larger question hanging over the discussion of instituting a stronger legal system: Is it possible to have rule of law in a one-party state? Although China's Communist Party has an internal disciplinary system, the Party's official status places it above the law. The Party itself cannot be sued, and a Communist Party member acting in an official capacity cannot even be sued in court. This could pose some juridical challenges for an aggrieved person. Certainly, the anomaly of trying to go through the difficult process of developing a rule-based society while providing an exemption from the rules for an important part of the society should be noted.

One thing is certain: despite the long process of WTO accession, during which important legal changes were made, China needs to accelerate its legal reform to bring the country into compliance with the WTO. Even Chinese experts themselves worry that the pace isn't fast enough.

"Lots of such work should have been done long ago," warned former MOFTEC vice-minister and lead WTO negotiator Tong Zhiguang in July 2001. "I am pretty worried about the current situation." He noted that anti-monopoly and anti-subsidy laws, two necessary pieces of legislation, hadn't been put into the National People's Congress legislation plan for the coming year.[4]

To their credit, many Chinese legal officials are acutely aware of the challenges ahead, and are willing to talk about them publicly, as was apparent at a seminar in Hong Kong at the end of 2000. "We ourselves are already very confused by WTO rules," said Wang Fei, a judge on the Shanghai High People's Court. "If we allow local courts to interpret [WTO rules], it will cause even more confusion." As a result, Wang noted that China is considering the possibility of dedicated tribunals for WTO cases so that judicial experts can rule on these complex issues. Wang and the two other judges at the seminar noted other problems. There are few precedents for how trade- and intellectual-property rights-related cases should be handled; there are inconsistencies in the awarding of compensation; there is a reluctance to allow the use of expert witnesses, for fear of offending other people in the field; and rules of evidence aren't well-defined. Warned Wang Fei: "If the Legislature does not strengthen our legal system after WTO accession we will have a hard time with TRIPS and it will be detrimental to the long-term protection of intellectual-property rights in China. We need judicial independence as well … After the accession to WTO there will be a judicial revolution in China … China will be a country ruled by law."[5]

TRADE AND HUMAN RIGHTS

Daunting though reforming even those parts of China's laws relating to trade and commerce is, it pales beside the challenge of bringing China into accordance with international human-rights standards. This book isn't intended to address in detail the troubling issue of the relationship between human rights and economic development. But no one interested in trade can ignore the question of what role, if any, freer trade and more open economies play in improving internationally recognized human rights as well as living conditions.

Chinese leaders frequently say that the most important human rights revolve around basic material needs, such as food and housing. By that standard, China has succeeded beyond even the most optimistic expectations, as the 200 million people who have been lifted out of absolute poverty since economic reforms began in 1978 can testify. The hundreds of millions more who have choices about where to work and where to live that their parents and grandparents could barely imagine are also a reflection of putting bread-and-butter issues ahead of other rights. These aren't trivial freedoms. Moreover, China isn't repressive in the sense that the former Soviet Union was. Take an example that is both simple and powerful in its contrast with the USSR: each year several million Chinese tourists travel abroad, securing passports with no more than the normal bureaucratic hassle that permeates everyday Chinese life. Since economic reforms began, 400,000 Chinese students have gone overseas to study, including the sons and daughters of many senior Chinese officials. They are building bridges between China and the outside world. Some of the returnees have started successful companies.

Many of these fledgling ventures are tech companies and a handful have even been listed on the US NASDAQ stock exchange.

Yet, because the overwhelming priority of China's leaders is stability, there is little if any commitment to ensuring that Chinese citizens enjoy other rights that are globally regarded as fundamental. These include freedom of belief, freedom of assembly, the right to a fair trial, and protection against torture and against arbitrary arrest and jailing. These are not so-called Western rights. These are universal rights. But they are violated all too frequently in China. Given the upheavals and tumult of the last century, it's easy to understand why China's leaders, and many of its people, want to avoid destabilizing change. But the systematic violation of basic human rights is both morally wrong and of doubtful value from the standpoint of development.

The respected international human-rights group Amnesty International contends that, despite economic progress, the human-rights situation in China has actually been deteriorating since 1998. Amnesty International professes special concern with an April 2001 decision to step up the "Strike Hard" anti-crime campaign. It contends that the decision resulted in tens of thousands of arrests and a record number of executions in the following weeks. From April until early July 2001, Amnesty International recorded 2960 death sentences and 1781 confirmed executions, "more in three months than in the rest of the world for the last three years". Amnesty International expresses concern over the speed with which the executions were carried out and observes that due legal process appears to be lacking in many cases. The group also cautions that, during this same period, China increased pressure on the *falun gong* spiritual movement (or, as the Chinese authorities prefer to call the group, "evil cult") and launched a new wave of arrests and forced repatriation of North Korean refugees. This repatriation apparently puts China in violation of the 1951 Refugee Convention, which it has ratified. No country is perfect but China's widespread human-rights violations and seeming lack of progress toward the standards laid out in the international agreements to which it is a party fuels critics who argue that freer trade doesn't lead to improved human rights and a more open society.[6]

Advocates of more open economies contend that freer trade and economic liberalization lead to political opening. While that is broadly true, it's difficult to point to a direct causal relationship. In China's case, it almost certainly will be decades before it comes close to approaching developed-country standards of human rights. The seeming lack of concern for international norms is deeply disturbing. Advocates of freer trade sometimes oversell the relationship between more open economies and more open societies. Despite almost a quarter-century of economic reform and equally sweeping social changes, those who anger Chinese authorities face a fate that can be every bit as grim as anything during the Maoist era. Despite many things that have changed for the better in China, true respect for fundamental human rights is a long way off. While the advocates of free trade and economic engagement are guilty of overpromising the benefits of openness, those who would somehow punish China for its transgressions haven't demonstrated that this policy, even if it were feasible, would pay off either. Almost invariably, the policy of economic isolation has failed. Economic opening and liberalization do pay off, if not as quickly or in quite the manner that human-rights advocates would like. Compare North Korea with China and there is no question which model is better for the country, for its people and for the world.

Indeed, even many human-rights activists don't advocate cutting China off from the world. "Broader trade with China can be consistent with advancing human rights, but only if it is combined with effective, sustained pressure on China to respect basic civil and political rights," testified Mike Jendrzejczyk, Washington Director of Human Rights Watch, in connection with a bill to grant China Permanent Normal Trading Relations status. "WTO membership in itself will not guarantee the rule of law, respect for worker rights, or meaningful political reform. Economic openness could be accompanied by tight restrictions on basic freedoms and a lack of governmental accountability. The Chinese government might seek to build the rule of law in the economic sphere while simultaneously continuing to pervert and undermine the rule of law elsewhere. For example, Chinese authorities claim to be upholding the 'rule of law' by arresting and throwing in jail pro-democracy activists, and the nationwide crackdown on the *falun gong* movement has been cloaked in rhetoric about the 'rule of law'."[7] Human Rights Watch contends that economic engagement should be accompanied by pressure on China to live up to international human-rights standards. This two-track approach has a greater chance of success than either naively expecting that market liberalization will inevitably lead to political change or imagining that isolating China will do anything to improve the well-being of the Chinese people.

GROWTH OF THE PRIVATE SECTOR

The growth in China's private sector has been extraordinary. Although private businesses only started after economic reforms began in 1978, the private sector now accounts for as much as two-thirds of economic activity, if the overwhelmingly private-sector agricultural economy is included. This development of the private sector in a nominally communist country occurred, as do so many of China's reforms, in a cautious, experimental fashion. Laws and regulations followed only after local governments and companies around the country gingerly attempted various forms of private enterprise. First came market-driven agriculture, which allowed peasants to freely sell anything above and beyond what they had contracted to supply the state. That innovation was followed by the formation of tiny private companies permitted to employ no more than eight people; larger-scale township and village enterprises followed, and now virtually everything is up for discussion as a possible private-sector component. As noted, even several of the largest state-owned companies, the country's crown jewels, have listed their shares on the New York and Hong Kong stock exchanges.

The private sector, and foreign-invested firms, are now China's economic drivers. According to a study by the International Finance Corporation (IFC), an arm of the World Bank, the output of private-sector firms grew by an average of 71% a year between 1991 and 1997. During the same period, employment at private companies grew by an average of 41% each year. The private sector has continued to develop rapidly since then. Both economic fundamentals and government policy are driving private-sector development. Dramatic growth in the private sector and a stagnant state-owned sector look to be features of the Chinese economic landscape that will endure for some time to come.

A turning point came at the 1997 Communist Party Congress, when delegates recognized private enterprise as an essential part of the economy. A constitutional amendment in 1999 affirmed that policy shift, lauded private companies as an "important component" of the economy and gave them the same status as their public counterparts in many important respects. The constitutional change gave an official seal of approval to a revolution that had been under way, in fits and starts, for more than two decades. Further changes have followed. For example, in 2000 the China Securities Regulatory Commission ended a quota system for initial public offerings. The quotas, which had been controlled by local governments, meant that politically favored companies were getting permission for stock-market listings while more entrepreneurial ones were not. Opening up stock-market financing for private companies should remove an important constraint on their ability to grow.

But, as in so many areas of the Chinese economy, big challenges still lie ahead. Because of continuing state control over so many aspects of life, it's misleading to imagine that an independent private sector of the sort that exists in more developed economies will develop any time in the foreseeable future. Private businesses all too often have an unhealthy symbiotic relationship with officials. Officials can make or break firms, by denying them licenses or showering them with preferential policies; local authorities can punish recalcitrant entrepreneurs with various taxes and fees or look the other way at tax evasion. Indeed, given the huge discretionary powers that Chinese officials wield, it's somewhat of a misnomer to call almost any but the smallest companies genuine private businesses. All too often, there is an unhealthy symbiotic relationship between businesses and government officials, forcing company executives to operate in a murky area.

For a glimpse of how this sort of pervasive discretionary power can be abused, consider the prospect of registering a business. It's a simple affair in developed economies, but not in China. One entrepreneur interviewed by the IFC recounted his travails in trying to register the name of a new restaurant. He wanted to open a restaurant with the name of "Paradise in the Real World". This name has four characters in Chinese, but the Bureau of Industry and Commerce asked that the name be changed to two or three characters. The entrepreneur proposed "The Paradise", but an official at the bureau retorted: "You are on the earth, so you cannot be registered as 'The Paradise'." The entrepreneur responded by saying that he assumed "The Real World" would be acceptable. "No," said the bureau official, "since we are all in the real world, that name is not appropriate, either." After several dinners and bribes, the entrepreneur eventually convinced the bureau that "Paradise in the Real World" was an acceptable name.[8] Stories like this are legion in China.

Financing is a nightmare. For all the many problems of the banking system, bankers show little inclination to be more innovative in lending. One Beijing-based entrepreneur, who exported Peking duck, explained to IFC staff the six steps he goes through to get a bank loan. First, he uses his business and social contacts to find a bank that will consider having him as a customer. Then he wines and dines bank executives. Next he provides extensive information to the credit committee. Then he woos a low-ranking branch loan officer. "Some officials may even ask [me] to buy a car or an apartment [for them]," he notes. Then he has to find a firm that will deposit money in the bank, for a fee, as collateral for his loan. Separately, he must pay a firm to provide a guarantee. All this is for a one-year loan, "and you have to worry about repayment by the end of the first half".[9] Not surprisingly, finance is at the heart of the weakness in China's system. It's depressingly predictable that banks are also at the center of much of the corruption that eats away at the Chinese system. Until there is a proper market-oriented financial system, it will be difficult to have confidence in the long-term sustainability of China's growth.

Trying to establish fair rules of the game and to see that they are implemented faithfully at the local level will be important in determining the ability of the private sector to thrive. It will also go a long way toward proving or disproving the success of the WTO regime in China, because the development of a rules-based system needed to nurture further development of the private sector dovetails with the changes needed to make WTO implementation a success in China. In turn, private entrepreneurs will also have to improve their game. Generally, even the largest companies are informally run, and are usually held together by a charismatic founder rather than a more durable management structure. There is little transparency even in the few cases of publicly listed private companies in China. Their accounting systems are usually primitive, designed as much to hide profits from authorities as to give a clear view of the business.

LOCAL PROTECTIONISM

Zealous officials intent on protecting home-grown industries are a big threat to continued economic development. Like everywhere else in the world, local businesses are a source not only of pride but of tax receipts and jobs as well. One of the WTO's biggest contributions may be in sweeping away the local favoritism that has long irked officials in Beijing. It's impossible to know how prevalent local protectionism is or how much of an impediment to growth it constitutes. But as China's economy becomes more sophisticated, and large-scale firms with the capacity to do business nationwide develop, it's almost certain that local barriers would take an increasingly significant bite out of the economy without pressure from an external source such as the WTO.

A telling incident that involved Shanghai, one of China's richest and most developed cities, deftly illustrates the need for reform. *Business China*, a Hong Kong-based newsletter that tracks the mainland economy, recounts the curious tale of how China's would-be financial center engaged in naked protectionism to help a locally based auto manufacturer. First, in mid-1998 the municipal government passed regulations to protect Santana cars. The cars are made in Shanghai in a joint venture between Volkswagen and the Shanghai Industry Automotive Corporation, a business that is one of the most profitable joint ventures in China. The regulations imposed extra licensing fees and sales taxes for cars that were produced outside of the city, adding as much as $9600 in extra costs for an "imported" car.

Shanghai wouldn't get its way without a fight. Up the Yangtze River from Shanghai, in the city of Wuhan, a competing joint venture between Citroen and local auto company Dong Feng Motor manufactures a car known as the Fukang. Provincial authorities were miffed that in the first half of 1999 their company only managed to sell 24 Fukangs in Shanghai, while 6400 Santanas were sold in Hubei province, where Wuhan is located. So Hubei authorities shot back with a variety of taxes that nearly doubled the cost of a Santana in Wuhan to $39,000.

Never mind that China has long prohibited these sorts of internal protectionist policies. In December 1999, Wu Shaohua, an official at the State Administration of Industrial Machinery, denounced this sort of "warlordism" that he said prevented the development of an integrated national auto industry. "China is a land torn apart by rival warlords," *Business China* quotes a Chinese economist who tracks the auto industry as saying. "If it is not Hubei against Shanghai, then it is the center against the localities."[10]

A cynic could be forgiven for wondering what difference the WTO will make. Yet the fact that an aggrieved foreign company can now petition its government to resolve a dispute of this sort through the WTO's dispute-resolution procedures may make local governments think twice before slapping on protectionist measures. It's but one tool, and it's certainly no magic wand. For instance, an aggrieved Chinese company wouldn't be able to take a case involving a domestic matter to the WTO, which is a multilateral forum where governments represent their companies' interests vis-à-vis other governments. In this case, Volkswagen or Citroen could have taken the case to their national governments and asked for WTO action, but their local partners alone would have been powerless to invoke WTO-specific protections. Their only hope in the future is that the domestic legal regime that accompanies accession to the WTO will prohibit this sort of local favoritism.

Although accession looms, China still has a long way to go in setting up the administrative framework to implement WTO procedures and ensure that its transparency requirements are met. There is a whole slew of areas where China is likely to implement changes more slowly than its foreign counterparts hope. Friction is almost certain in telecommunications and finance, where bureaucratic latitude remains high even with the advent of WTO status. And it's hard to imagine that all sorts of technical barriers to trade, such as procedures for agricultural imports, will disappear overnight. They never do. Technology-transfer requirements and local-content standards are so deeply ingrained in the minds of many officials that these, too, won't disappear easily. In fact, if not in law, they are likely to remain in some form.

Despite optimism about the beneficial effect of WTO membership for China, the difficulties it will mean for individual companies, and even entire industries, cannot be overemphasized. Many sectors are heavily subsidized and their international competitiveness is doubtful. The troubled financial sector is the most obvious problem point. But cement, automobiles, steel and agriculture, to take but some of the most obvious examples, all rely on heavy state support in the form of preferential policies and loans, as well as outright protectionism.

Agriculture

Agriculture was one of the most sensitive issues in China's accession negotiations. That sensitivity was no surprise, given that some 900 million of China's 1.3 billion people live in rural areas. About 400 million people, or more than half of all employed people, are farmers. They are already slipping behind their more prosperous urban compatriots and are showing increasing signs of restiveness. Politically, the government couldn't afford to look like it was ignoring the needs of farmers in the WTO accession talks, given the rural sector's large population and the central place peasants have occupied in the political history of revolutionary China. Chinese negotiators won the right to give heavier subsidies, up to 8.5% of the total production value, to the agricultural sector than the US would have liked. Still, there were major concessions to foreign interests. Agricultural tariffs will drop to an average of 17% and even lower (14.5%) for US priority products such as pork, poultry, citrus, wine and cheese. Tariffs on grapes will fall, from 40% before the accord to 13% after WTO entry; tariffs on wine imports will fall from 65% to 20%. Non-tariff barriers, which often allow for erratic import policies, will be replaced by scientific import regulations.

Good news though the lower tariffs will undoubtedly be for American and other export-oriented farmers abroad, they also reflect a welcome, and potentially radical, re-thinking of China's policy of agricultural self-sufficiency. For decades, China has succeeded in feeding itself. Now, the amount of arable cropland per head is shrinking and environmental degradation is increasing, as more marginal land is pressed into service to produce crops. Reflecting the rising cost that the policy of self-sufficiency in grain demands, the government now requires that domestic producers supply only 95% of domestic grain needs, down from 100% not long ago.

This cautious move away from self-sufficiency is the

thin end of a wedge that is likely to see less official interest in commodity products such as rice and more emphasis on higher value-added crops, such as fruits and vegetables. The move away from the creed of self-sufficiency might presage the removal of the clumsy grain management system. In mid-2001, Vice-Premier Wen Jiabao said that China would experiment with a free-market system for grain in selected areas.[11] The current grain management system guarantees farmers a set price for their grain (usually above market prices), yet hasn't succeeded in making them happy because it strips them of the freedom to grow higher value-added crops. On top of that, the system has been inefficient and riddled with corruption. It's a system that, whatever its past virtues, needs to be re-thought. WTO accession may help provide the push that authorities need to overhaul the regime. Indirectly, the WTO will accelerate moves to give farmers greater security over their land. One significant change under consideration is to give farmers 60-year leases, twice the standard current length.

Re-thinking agriculture will have tremendous spill-over effects. As people are freed from the land, they will flock to towns and cities. The long-standing restrictions on free movement, known as the *hukou* system, are already being questioned. They are likely to be slowly revised over the coming decade. China is going to be an agricultural country for many years to come, but the WTO will speed up the transition to a more urban one. Already, the agricultural workforce has shrunk dramatically. It was three-quarters of the working population when economic reforms began in 1978; now it's just 45%. In the US, with its enormously productive agricultural sector, fewer than 3% of workers are in agriculture. While China is unlikely ever to drop anywhere near this level, rural-urban migration will continue at a rapid rate for decades to come. This will be a powerful force to drive economic growth, as workers in the manufacturing and service sectors are almost invariably more productive than those on small farms that rely largely on manual labor.

Finance

Financial reform is a prerequisite for continued high economic growth. And it's one of the areas on which WTO entry will have the most impact. China's under-developed banks and brokers will face steadily increased foreign competition as a result of specific and wide-ranging agreements negotiated under the WTO accession accord. In finance, as in many other areas, change is already under way. But finance is among the most politically charged areas of the economy and one of the most difficult to make market-oriented; it's through control of the financial system that Chinese leaders continue to bend the economy to their will. WTO agreement or no, it remains to be seen whether China truly embraces a more market-oriented system or keeps its financial system subservient to political control.

Certainly, the promises that China made as part of the accession agreement are extraordinary. Two years after accession, foreign banks will be able to conduct local-currency business with Chinese companies; after five years, they will be able to set up accounts for ordinary Chinese retail customers. Foreign firms will be able to buy one-third stakes in asset-management companies (AMCs) and investment banks immediately upon accession and raise that share to 49% after three years. Most strikingly, foreign banks will enjoy so-called national treatment within five years — in other words, they will have the privileges that domestic banks enjoy. No favoritism can be shown to either domestic or foreign banks. Chinese banks will, for the first time, face real competition.

On paper, China has a fairly well-developed financial system, one that has exploded in size and sophistication since reform began. Its four leading commercial banks rank among the world's largest when measured by assets. Savings are high and loans outstanding are a little over $1 trillion, or about the same size as annual GDP. That volume reflects a well-developed credit market but a society that isn't drowning in debt. Securities markets have developed rapidly since they were established (or, in the case of Shanghai, re-established) in 1990. With a combined market capitalization of $600 billion, the Shenzhen and Shanghai stock exchanges together are already larger than Hong Kong's exchange. Growth in many kinds of financial products, from mutual funds to life insurance, has been high in the past decade.

Yet, the reality is that this is a primitive, politicized financial system, whose players will have trouble competing against world-class financial institutions. Simply by virtue of its size, the biggest problems lie in the banking sector. Lending is dominated by four large banks — the Industrial and Commercial Bank of China, the Bank of China, the China Construction Bank and the Agricultural Bank of China. Together, they account for about two-thirds of all loans in China. Traditionally, the banks have collected deposits from individual savers and lent them to state-owned enterprises. Unfortunately, the state-owned enterprises all too often made investments on the basis of state plans, or no plan whatsoever, rather than on market principles. The result has been predictably disastrous. A typical case: China Construction Bank lent money for the construction of a railroad from a coal mine to a power plant some 100 kilometers away. The bank duly lent the necessary money so that the railroad could be built as part of the country's planned economy. Unfortunately, the power plant, though it was inked into the plan, was never built. The railroad is completely unviable economically without the power plant, so the bank ended up with a non-performing loan.

As bad debts like this mounted, China's leaders decided to split off the purely policy banks — those which would serve a development role — from the commercial banks. In 1994, the government formed three development-oriented banks. The remaining Big Four were supposed to make loans on a commercial basis. It hasn't worked out that way. Indeed, the rate of bad loans may even have accelerated following that split. Many of the Big Four invested in wildly speculative property projects throughout the boom of the early and mid-1990s. During the fever of property speculation during the 1990s, the government remained largely powerless to halt lending that was occurring outside the central plan.

As the economy grew, abusive financing practices, usually involving loans to powerful local officials, began to be a regular feature of the increasing number of publicly reported corruption cases. Indeed, banks are at the center of much of the country's widespread corruption problem, because bribes grease the way for loans that often turn into non-performing ones. The National Audit Office estimated that two of the country's Big Four banks, the Industrial and Commercial Bank of China and the China Construction

Bank, had each lost $1.2 billion through illegal activities.[12] Premier Zhu Rongji has threatened stiff penalties for bank officers involved in irregular lending. A central bank mandate in the mid-1990s to cut non-performing loans by two to three percentage points a year also put the Big Four under pressure. It's too early to say whether these have had the intended effect. The measures have, apparently, made bankers more reluctant to extend credit. Liquidity has piled up in Chinese banks in recent years, but there's no evidence that it has made them more likely to lend money on the basis of commercial practices.

Probably no one, not even Chinese officials, really knows how large China's non-performing loans are. Central bank Governor Dai Xianglong has said that around one-quarter of all loans have some problems. But Chinese officials have released little detailed information on the size of the non-performing loans, let alone enough data to make meaningful comparisons over time or to distinguish between loans that will have to be written off completely and those that are experiencing temporary difficulties. It's not clear whether Chinese authorities are concerned about spooking depositors and provoking a potentially destabilizing bank run, are worried about the embarrassment of fully disclosing how serious the bad-debt situation is, are indulging in a traditional penchant for secrecy or honestly don't have a grip on the problem. On top of that, writing off bad debts reduces reported profits and thus means lower taxes. Thus, the Ministry of Finance opposes large debt write-downs.

Independent analysts generally estimate that about 40% of loans are troubled, but estimates go as high as 75%. In early 2001, the Bank of China released bad-loan figures that showed that non-performing loans accounted for 28.8%

of its portfolio in 1999, more than double what it had previously calculated using different criteria. Although the high level of non-performing debts makes the bank technically insolvent, rating agencies and analysts viewed the move positively because it represented one of the first signs that management at a major Chinese bank was serious about coming to grips with the bad-debt issue. Whatever the exact number, every serious analyst agrees that the non-performing loan problem must be dealt with more forcefully in order to put China's banks on a sounder financial footing and help them prepare for economic growth and market opening.[13]

China took a step toward cleaning up the problem when it established asset-management companies in 1999. Similar to the Resolution Trust Corporation in the United States, which took loans from failed thrift institutions, China's asset-management companies were set up in an effort to do away once and for all with the overhang of bad debts. Unlike the US, where a single institution took all the bad debts, a dedicated asset-management corporation was set up to take non-performing loans from each of the Big Four banks. For example, Huarong Asset Management took the Industrial and Commercial Bank of China's bad loans, and China Cinda (also known as Xinda) Asset Management took China Construction Bank's dud loans. The Agricultural Bank and the Bank of China also have their own asset-management units. Although nominally independent, these are for the most part staffed with people who formerly worked at the respective banks.

Initial assessments of the AMCs' performance are mixed. There have been a number of debt-for-equity swaps, which have allowed companies that have successful operating businesses to clean up their balance sheets by reducing debt and raising equity. However, management often remains reluctant to give its new equity holder, the bank, a real say in running the companies. It's also unclear if the banks or AMCs have the expertise to play the sort of powerful board role that German banks (to take the best analogy) exercise vis-à-vis the companies in which they hold substantial stakes.

Moreover, the AMCs have been slow to sell assets. Management, following a government directive to get at least a 30% recovery rate on the loans, seems preoccupied with getting a high price. In the case of the Resolution Trust Corporation, the emphasis was on getting assets into the hands of someone who could use them productively. In China, there seems to be a concern with minimizing the headline loss, rather than looking at the long-term (and less measurable) cost of sub-par assets that are a drain on both banks and, ultimately, taxpayers. That loss is compounded if those assets could be used more productively. Nicholas Lardy, a scholar at the Brookings Institution and an expert on China's financial system, thinks that a financial crisis is likely. He notes that bad loans continue to mount, that the asset-management companies aren't doing their job and that there are few signs of reforming the traditional credit culture. Lardy thinks that bad debts could be equivalent to 75% of GDP. By comparison, the traumatic US Savings and Loan crisis during the 1980s ended up costing about 3% of GDP.[14]

The issue of the bad loans and their resolution is critical for several reasons. Most immediately, of course, they are a burden on the Chinese financial system. They slow down economic growth, sucking up resources that could be used more productively. They will also cost the Chinese taxpayer large sums of money. And the longer the problem festers, the higher the ultimate bill. But bad loans also highlight issues of policy-making credibility and transparency in China's economy. Cleaning up the bad loans has become a major test of China's ability to get its economic house in order. It has done this, to date, with minimal transparency and mixed results.

Finally, the biggest test will be whether or not Chinese banks have the ability to adopt more modern credit practices. Will politically oriented lending end? Can Chinese banks wean themselves from lending based on personal relationships? Can bankers learn how to do real, fundamental credit analysis? This will be the ultimate test of whether China's banking system can compete.

Banks and regulators are making the right noises. Most of the Big Four banks are headed by relatively young, reform-minded chief executives. They are acutely aware of the challenges they face, both generally and as a result of WTO accession, and they've initiated a variety of programs to make their institutions more market-oriented. Central authorities are pushing ahead with ambitious plans to list Chinese state-owned banks on foreign stock exchanges. The first listing, expected in 2002, will likely be the Bank of China's Hong Kong operations. Interestingly, these operations account for the bulk of the bank's profitability. The hope is to allow other banks to list abroad. More importantly, once a secure foundation is established, policy makers and bank executives intend to inject mainland operations (such as the Beijing or Shanghai branches) into the listed company. As with the energy and telecommunications companies, this listing strategy could have far-reaching results. Listings will provide capital; at least as important, they will provide oversight from institutional investors.

Telecommunications

China's telecommunications world presents a paradox: It's one of the fastest-growing sectors of the economy, yet it remains firmly under government control. A system of managed competition has made China's telecommunications markets one of the world's largest and fastest-growing in just 10 years. In 1990, telephones were still a rarity, with only six lines for every 1000 people. The whole country only had about seven million phone lines. There were long waiting lists to get new lines and, without *guanxi*, a new line installation took years. People wanting to make a telephone call typically lined up at street-corner kiosks. An aggressive building program has changed all that. In a triumph of state planning and successful technology transfer from abroad, China installed almost 140 million additional fixed telephone lines during the 1990s.

The growth of the wireless telephone business is even more astounding. In July 2001, China surpassed the US to claim the title of having more mobile subscribers than any country in the world — 120.6 million at the end of the month. The number of subscribers has been increasing by tens of millions a year. As recently as the end of 1999 there were only 43 million subscribers. A pair of companies, China Mobile and China Unicom, both of which have listed their shares on the New York and Hong Kong stock exchanges, account for the majority of subscribers.

Yet for all its dynamism, the telecommunications sector also is one of the most heavily controlled. A conservative

Ministry of Information Industry, headed by Minister Wu Jichuan, has been focused on building up a handful of national champions and denying the fruits of the Chinese market to foreigners. At the end of 2000, he and other ministry officials confirmed foreign investors' fears of policy opacity when they allowed a report of an important policy change that purportedly was issued by the ministry to fester uncorrected for days. Investors had been spooked by a news story that the Ministry of Information Industry would change the billing method that cellular-telephone companies were allowed to use. The change would mean that the person receiving a call would no longer have to pay for air time. This change would have important implications for revenues and profitability, and worried investors hammered the stock prices of China Mobile and China Unicom.

When Wu finally did stand up to correct the record, he showed why investing in China is a risky business. Investors in China should check with him, he admonished, before selling their shares. He conveniently ignored the fact that the purported leak came from his ministry. Neither he nor anyone at the ministry would clarify the remark in the days between the report and his press conference. "There are many opinions," he said. "But what matters is mine."

The controversy over the billing practice is telling for two reasons. First, the fact that the government, rather than a pair of New York Stock Exchange-listed companies, can unilaterally and without consultation decide on tariff rates and billing policies shows the continuing intense involvement of the state in the Chinese economy. (In fairness, the state owns a majority stake in both of these companies; it acts, however, as if it still owns all of them.)

The incident was yet another reminder of how far China has to go before its private market breaks free of heavy-handed government interference. Second, the imbroglio underscored how these state-sponsored anti-competitive practices can hurt consumers. After all, the idea of letting consumers receive calls free of charge is standard practice in most countries and the principle that companies should be able to compete to win customers is fundamental to a market economy.

Yet Wu's policy of nurturing state-owned companies has unquestionably paid big dividends so far. Thanks to the protection it enjoys in the world's fastest-growing market, China Mobile topped *BusinessWeek*'s list of emerging-market companies in both 2000 and 2001. The list, compiled by Morgan Stanley Capital International, ranks emerging-market companies on the basis of market capitalization. Even though China Mobile suffered from the plunge in telecommunications stocks and from fears that it had already creamed off the most profitable users and thus had little room for continued rapid growth, in mid-2001 its market capitalization stood at an impressive $90 billion. Profits in 2000 nearly quadrupled to $2.2 billion on sales of $7.8 billion. China's other major mobile operator, China Unicom, weighed in at number eight on the list following its 2000 initial public offering. By the time foreign telecom companies hook up with local rivals, China Mobile and China Unicom will be well entrenched.

Automobiles

Because of the large role that automobiles occupy in most economies, this is an industry to which Chinese and foreign negotiators paid keen attention during WTO negotiations.

The result will have significant implications for investment and employment. There are now more than 100 automobile and truck assemblers throughout China. Most of these are decidedly small-scale, low-tech affairs. But they tend to be big business for many of the cities where they are located. The incident mentioned in the earlier section on local protectionism, which involved two of the country's largest auto makers, shows just how contentious the issue can be.

As matters stand now, the foreign auto sector is tightly restricted. First, companies need an import license. Then they have to contend with high tariffs, which can double the cost of a car. (Still, even the pre-WTO tariffs of 80–100% in 2001 were a big improvement from the levels of nearly 200% not too much earlier.) Foreign companies cannot actually do the importing, but must use a state firm — so General Motors (GM) or Ford cannot import its own cars. Nor can they sell those cars (they must use independent retailers), provide financing to buy the cars, or even help to ensure that their customers are satisfied with their purchases by engaging in any form of after-sales service.[15]

On top of that, foreign auto makers face other barriers. Chinese authorities strong-armed companies that have set up manufacturing operations in the country, including GM, into localizing more of their production, especially in the components area, than they otherwise would have chosen. That meant they have had to provide a good deal of know-how in the form of technology transfer. And they have been subjected to balancing requirements, where their ability to obtain foreign exchange to finance imports is tied to export volumes. GM and other foreign auto makers also have faced strict limitations on setting up new factories. Foreign companies cannot own more than 50% of an auto-manufacturing venture, and they must get government approval to make one model rather than another. In GM's case, the Detroit auto maker spent almost $2 billion on an auto factory in Shanghai and related component-manufacturing investments. Yet it had to accede to Chinese requests that it manufacture Buicks, hardly the car of choice for most Chinese buyers. Only later did it win approval for a more marketable family wagon. In a final twist, underscoring just how political the project was, the final contract signing for the Shanghai plant didn't occur until then-US Vice President Al Gore agreed to appear with Chinese Premier Li Peng at a ceremonial banquet.

The WTO agreement will usher in some big changes. Tariffs will fall from the current 80–100% to 25% over the five years following WTO entry. Tariffs on auto parts will be cut to an average of 10% within six years. Import licenses will be more generous and will be phased out entirely five years after accession. Distribution, retail and after-service will be opened up immediately to foreign investment, with foreign companies allowed to take a majority stake after the second year. China will eliminate all restrictions on foreign-invested companies importing and exporting within three years of accession, ending what General Motors China Vice Chairman and General Counsel Tim Stratford says has been a "nightmare" for GM.

Foreign auto companies will be able to finance autos, a measure that should give a big boost to sales in a country where bank finance even for companies is limited and consumer credit virtually non-existent. The current requirements regarding local content, technology transfer and exports will be eliminated at the time of accession. Joint-venture producers will also have more freedom to introduce new models and new vehicles. Central-government approval won't be needed for investments of up to $100 million. "We think it's one of the most exciting things that's happened since China opened up to the world in 1978," says Stratford.

&   &   &

Clearly, foreign companies will be among the big winners in the Chinese economy. But China's economy is a vast continental one. It won't be dominated by foreign companies the way a city-state's such as Singapore is. China has a solid base of manufacturing companies, some of which will thrive amidst the new competitive pressure. It has a good technical base. And with China's vast domestic market, foreign companies will put in both manufacturing and research-and-development facilities more readily than they would in most other developing countries.

But it's China's people, and its economy, who will be the biggest winners. Certainly, economic reform has already brought many losers, and it will be imperative that the government does what it can to help those who are left behind. Educational and health-care opportunities are diminishing for the poor and it's important that the social safety net be repaired. Political support for economic and trade liberalization could evaporate if inequality continues to rise. But if China can manage to get through what will undoubtedly be a very difficult transition period, its future will be more secure than at any time in the last several centuries. Accession to the WTO will act to cut the knots that have bound the economy. The costly ties between banks and state-owned enterprises should dissolve, as many of the subsidies that prop up uncompetitive firms will be outlawed and banks will be forced to make market-oriented decisions. The unhealthy links between government officials and business people will be dissolved in favor of the bonds of an increasingly rule-based society. External pressure will provide much of the motive power as a quarter-century of internally driven reforms loses momentum. This, at least, is the hope of China's leaders.

　　　　　🐾　　🐾　　🐾

WTO PRINCIPLES AS THEY RELATE TO CHINA

National Treatment: Once goods have cleared customs, there can be no discrimination against foreign goods, in terms of taxation or other treatment. Laws and regulations cannot favor local goods at the expense of foreign ones.

Ban on Quantitative Restriction on Imports and Exports: The WTO aims to make import duties the only form of trade restriction. This makes the process more predictable and more transparent.

Transparency:
Publication: Laws, regulations, administrative rules and judicial decisions related to trade must be published promptly so that governments and traders can become acquainted with them. Government measures that will result in increased burdens should be officially published before they are enforced. These must be administered in a "uniform, impartial and reasonable manner".

　　Review Process: There must be a review process (such as courts or administrative tribunals) to review objectively (and, if necessary, correct) administrative actions related to customs matters.

Information Availability: A national point for inquiries, which can respond to questions from other members regarding technical regulations, standards and conformity-assessment procedures, has been established.

60-day Notification Period: The WTO must be notified at least 60 days before the adoption of new technical measures and procedures if they are not the same as international standards and may have a significant effect on the trade of other WTO members.

Local-government Compliance: The central government must take "reasonable measures" (defined as "serious, persistent and convincing efforts") to ensure that local governments comply with WTO rules.

Subsidies: Export subsidies and import-substitution subsidies are banned altogether. Subsidies to state-owned enterprises ended in 2000.

What's Prohibited: Discrimination against goods or services from another member country or a domestic producer. Measures requiring local sourcing are out. So too are trade-balancing requirements, which require that an enterprise's imports are tied to its exports or its foreign-exchange requirements.

China has agreed not to require technology-transfer agreements, local content or production offsets.[16]

1   Warwick McKibbin, "China and the WTO: Some empirical results", cited in Yiping Huang, "WTO Entry: China's Boon, Asia's Bane?", in Salomon Smith Barney, *Asian Economics: Outlook and Strategy*, June 2001, pp. 13–14 (mimeo).

2   The Wolfensohn remarks are from a July 9, 2001 speech, cited at http://wbln0018.worldbank.org/news/pressrelease.nsf/673fa6c5a2d50a67852565e200692a79/34a92ea3463e57eb85256a840041d3ea?OpenDocument

3   These figures are from the English-language edition of the official *People's Daily*, September 29, 2000. The paper noted that tax revenue as a percentage of China's GDP has been rising steadily. In 1995, tax revenue made up just 2% of GDP. The figure was expected to rise to 14% in 2000. The central government's share of total tax revenue surged from 20% in 1993 to an estimated 58% in 2000. Subsequently, on January 4, 2001, *People's Daily* reported that 2000 tax revenues were 14.2% of GDP.

4   "WTO Laws in Deadline Race" and "Champion of WTO Entry" by Liu Weiling and Sun Min, *China Daily*, July 27, 2001. The remark wasn't made in response to Zhang's statement but in reference to the anti-monopoly and anti-subsidy legislation.

5   The seminar was sponsored by Hong Kong's Legal Education Trust Fund and took place on December 16, 2001.

6   The quotes come from Amnesty International, "China's Execution Frenzy", p. 1, at www.web.amnesty.org/web/wire.nsf/september2001/china. For the more general information, see "Human Rights in China in 2001 — A New Step Backwards", September 3, 2001, on the Amnesty International website, Index number ASA 170282001.

7   The testimony was given on February 16, 2000. See www.hrw.org/campaigns/china-99/china-testimony0216.htm.

8   International Finance Corporation, *China's Emerging Private Enterprises*, Washington, D.C., International Finance Corporation, 2000, p. 65.

9   *Ibid.*, p. 56.

10   This incident was described in "Car Wars", *Business China*, January 4, 2000.

11   Dian Tai, "Grain to go on a free market price system: Wen", *China Daily*, August 22, 2001.

12   This was quoted in "The Golden Fleece", *Business China*, March 12, 2001. It's not clear what period this is for or what activities made up the losses. As with so much in the Chinese economy, we have only fragmentary information. But we can see enough to understand the general picture.

13   The release of the Bank of China's non-performing debt figure and its implications was covered extensively in a series of articles by James Kynge in the *Financial Times*: "China bad debt higher than thought", May 12,

2001; "Beijing aims to tackle banking weakness", May 13, 2001; "Governor Liu increases pressure to clean out the stables", May 16, 2001; "Loans move turns up heat on 'big four'", May 16, 2001.

[14] Nicholas R. Lardy, "China's Worsening Debts", *Financial Times*, June 22, 2001. Our comparison with the US is somewhat misleading because that represents the net cost; the estimate that bad loans equal 75% of GDP doesn't take into account the fact that some of those loans won't turn sour and that money will be recovered on some of them. Still, the picture is clearly not promising. If bad loans ultimately cost the equivalent of 25–50% of annual economic output, as now seems likely, China's will rank as one of the biggest bad-debt burdens in modern economic history.

[15] Adapted from a presentation given by Tim Stratford, General Motors China Vice Chairman and General Counsel, at the American Chamber of Commerce, Hong Kong, January 10, 2001. All Stratford's remarks in this chapter are from the seminar.

[16] *Ibid*.

CHAPTER 6

Making Globalization and the WTO Work for All

C hina joins the WTO at a crucial time both for the young organization and for the future of the liberal, open trading system that has underpinned more than a half-century of unparalleled global growth and prosperity. Globalization and an open trading system, the very source of this golden age, are under unprecedented attack. East Asia and, above all, China have shown remarkable progress in using globalization, epitomized by greater trade, to reduce poverty. The 200 million people in China who have been lifted out of poverty since reforms began are one of the most powerful arguments that economic reform and opening pays real dividends in people's lives. If China's WTO accession goes well, it will be a powerful argument for the benefits of the global trading order and its ability to help countries develop.

Conversely, if WTO accession and the economic changes it galvanizes go badly, a country that should stand as a symbol of everything that globalization can achieve will stand, instead, as a monument to its failed promise. In China, if WTO status exacerbates underlying economic problems, a worst-case scenario could see catastrophic events for the country, ones that could damage the region and even the world. More narrowly for the WTO, in the years following accession China could damage what is still a young organization finding its way and trying to establish its authority. Because China's WTO entry comes at a time of heightened doubts about globalization, it's especially important that the entry goes smoothly. Creative thinking will be needed to ensure a smooth transition. More broadly, we need to ensure that the WTO works for development, in China and around the world.

The Asian economic crisis, the wrenching transformation that Russia and many of the other former "socialist" economies have undergone, and a series of meltdowns in emerging markets such as Argentina and Turkey have prompted increasing numbers of critics to question the whole process of globalization. The world has become measurably richer over the past half-century. But, understandably, there's impatience at the speed with which development has (and hasn't) occurred and the unevenness of its progress. Unfairly, globalization has shouldered the blame for all manner of economic and social ills, such as a purported widening gap between rich and poor, deepening poverty and excessive indebtedness in some countries, environmental degradation, widening trade and current-account deficits, rising joblessness, and even violations of labour and human rights. If its proponents cannot articulate the case for globalization, the world could be doomed to perpetuate a vicious cycle of trade retaliation that would mean serious disruption and dislocation. Hopefully, China's entry into the WTO should show more powerfully than any other example the benefits of liberal trade and development policies.

Throughout the world, as in China, there must be a

concerted effort to see that more of globalization's benefits go to the poor. This is a moral imperative and a political necessity. If globalization mostly helps those who are already more or less well-off, the resulting backlash could be disastrous for the entire global order. But it's more globalization, not less, that represents the best way to deal with issues ranging from the environmental problems of the developing world to the extreme poverty that today oppresses 1.2 billion people. It must be a more nuanced version of globalization than we have seen during the past two decades. A naïve belief that more liberalization of any sort is better and that, left to themselves, markets will simply solve the problem of global poverty has been proven wrong. Moreover, this ideology-driven approach to liberalization isn't going to work politically in a world riven by a debate over the costs of globalization.

We need to articulate more forcefully the degree to which globalization has helped development and improved people's lives. Real progress *has* been made. Since the 1960s, life expectancy in developing countries has jumped from 46 to 64 years, while infant mortality rates have been halved. Twice as many people now have clean drinking water and basic sanitation services. The proportion of children enrolled in primary school has jumped 80%. But even the progress in the past four decades in the developing world isn't enough.[1]

Too many people are desperately poor in a world of plenty. One of every five people in the world now lives in extreme poverty. Two-thirds of these 1.2 billion people are women. They live without enough food, without clean water and sanitation, without education. That can, and must, change. The globalization agenda must be broadened to include the eradication of poverty. There are achievable poverty-reduction goals embodied in a visionary effort known as the International Development Targets to dramatically reduce poverty over the next decade. During the 1990s, many governments of the world and international organizations (including the World Bank and the IMF) agreed to these proposals. These aims represent a program that is both bold and achievable. The targets are:

- To halve the number of people living in abject poverty by 2015.
- To provide universal primary education by 2015.
- To eliminate discrimination against girls in primary and secondary education by 2005.
- To reduce infant and child mortality by two-thirds and maternal mortality by three-quarters by 2015.
- To provide access to reproductive-health services for all who need it by no later than 2015.
- To ensure that current trends in environmental destruction are reversed, at both the global and national levels, by 2015.

Rallying around these goals would be a simple way of demonstrating the promise of globalization and building bridges between developing and developed countries, between globalization skeptics and those who hold more traditional views. Achieving this level of poverty reduction will require a real commitment by leaders in both the developed and developing world. But it would be just the sort of dramatic statement that the world needs at a time when globalization is under attack.

THE CHINA CHALLENGE: WTO AND BEYOND

No country in history has burst onto the world trading stage like China. It was less than a quarter-century ago, in December 1978, that Chinese leaders first adopted their initial economic reform program. That year China's exports were a paltry $9.75 billion. Since then, they have increased more than 25-fold. By 2000, when it racked up exports of $250 billion, China was exporting every two weeks what it had sent abroad in all of 1978. China now accounts for 4% of world trade and ranks as the world's seventh-largest exporter. Like foreign direct investment and, it seems, just about everything else in China's economy, exports look set to keep growing. The World Bank predicts a big jump in trade, with China accounting for 6.3% of global exports by 2005.[2] Without WTO membership its share of world trade would only increase modestly, to around 4.5%.

Significantly, the Bank estimates that imports as well as exports will grow dramatically as a result of WTO accession and that the trade account will be close to balanced. China looks unlikely to follow the neo-mercantilist model that critics accused Japan and South Korea of practicing so assiduously, a system that aided exporters but was unfriendly to imports and thus provoked international trade tensions. A look at China's wide-ranging tariff cuts shows the country's commitment to liberalization. Tariffs have plummeted, from an average of 42.9% as recently as 1992 to 15% in 2001. Under the WTO they'll fall further, to 9.4% by 2005. To put it simply, high tariffs no longer are the problem. Another indication of the commitment to change can be seen in the ability of the US to negotiate an average tariff rate of just 7.1% for what it deemed to be priority products. On top of that, China has promised to implement the Information Technology Agreement, which will eliminate tariffs for a variety of IT products by 2005, compared to the 13.3% average level prevailing in 2001.

❧   ❧   ❧

China is a rising power. Rising powers are inevitably disruptive to the existing order. The role that it will play in the WTO will be an important indication of China's stance as it inches toward big-power status. Will China be a status-quo power or will it be more assertive, redrawing rules for its own benefit? Since its opening began more than two decades ago, China has largely been a free rider in organizations like the United Nations. It hasn't been a major contributor in terms of people or resources. But it hasn't acted to frustrate the ambitions of current powers either. Despite differences with the US, China's stance is very different from that of the former Soviet Union, which pursued a confrontational stance toward the US and Western Europe in the United Nations and many other international bodies. However, China's economic might won't automatically translate into political power. Notably, although Japan has started to take more of a leadership role in Asia since the onset of the economic crisis, Japan hasn't developed political clout to match its status as the world's second-largest economy. So even if China does emerge as an economic superpower over the next decade or two, that's not enough to guarantee that it will be an international political heavyweight, willing and able to project power on a global basis. To date, China's stance has been uncompromising on only a few issues, most notably its claims to sovereignty over Taiwan.

Yet there are signs that China will play a more assertive role, at least economically, and that could have consequences for the WTO and other bodies. China first showed signs of a more activist regional policy during the Asian financial crisis. First, it dipped into its foreign-exchange reserves to donate $1 billion as part of the IMF's $17.3 billion rescue package for Thailand in August 1997. This was an unprecedented example of regional cooperation on China's part and came at a time when the United States pointedly declined to help because of the mistaken belief that the crisis that began in Thailand was of little import. Then, despite a round of devaluations, Chinese leaders spurned the pleas of domestic exporters and refused to devalue their currency. Other than the Hong Kong dollar, which has a rigid peg to the US dollar through a currency board system, China's was the only major currency in the East Asian region that held its value during the 1997–98 crisis. That courageous decision to hold firm hurt Chinese exports and the Chinese economy in 1998. But it helped arrest the contagion. It also won thanks from Asian and US leaders.

Since the Asian crisis, China also has taken a prominent role in the region's two most significant economic initiatives. The more important of the two is the so-called Chiang Mai initiative, whereby governments of the region have pledged to use their reserves to defend each other's currencies in case of speculative attacks. China has also emerged as a supporter of moves toward the long-term goal of a regional currency union. That would be coupled with the sort of economic integration that has occurred in Europe with the introduction of a single currency, the

Euro. Such a move for Asia is many decades off, at least, but China's willingness to take part in discussions on the topic nonetheless marks a notable indication of its intentions to play a more assertive role. Reflecting China's increasing economic power and prominence, it may not be too early to consider a G-9 Summit, with China joining the Group of Eight (G-8) as the newest member.

If China follows through on the private signals it has sent that it intends to play an important role in the WTO, it could have an extremely positive impact on the organization. China has the political and economic power, as well as the credibility of a developing country, to be an important bridge between the developed and developing world. China is unlikely to join any formal blocs, such as the so-called Like-Minded Countries, an informal grouping that includes India and Brazil and the most important representative of developing countries' interests at the WTO. But it will help to balance the dominance of what is known as the Quad, a grouping that includes the US, Japan, the European Union and Canada. However, China's role and its intentions will only be truly tested during a new round of trade negotiations.

For the rest of Asia, China's economic rise and its accession to the WTO is a resounding wake-up call. China's full and transparent participation in the multilateral trading system should have many positive spin-offs. Sustainable growth in China should boost world trade volumes. Sharper competition may spur much-needed reforms in the rest of Asia. If their companies rise to the challenge, Asian countries will be among the biggest beneficiaries of this increased volume, which would be particularly welcome given the anemic state of the Japanese economy. Stronger intra-regional trade, if it occurs, will help give the region more autonomy from the swings of the European and US markets. The ASEAN economies of Southeast Asia will be brought into a closer economic partnership with China, Japan and South Korea.

The region won't automatically reap the benefits of China's growth and openness. It must accelerate reforms. Top priority should go to completing introduction of the ASEAN Free-Trade Area, which allows for virtually duty-free access among the 10 countries of the region by 2005. Malaysia must allow its automotive industry to be subject to the agreement. After all, a loss of competitiveness won't be to other ASEAN members but to China. Member countries should also accelerate completion of the ASEAN Investment Area, which allows for freer investment in the region, by moving up the start date to 2005 from the current 2008. Closer ties with China, Japan and South Korea (the so-called ASEAN+3) should be established. To encourage outward investments from China, concrete steps to work toward an Asian Economic Community should be institutionalized as soon as possible.

&. &. &.

Besides the geo-strategic issue of what role the world's newest emerging power will play, there are a host of smaller WTO-specific issues that will go a long way to determining China's impact. Without a doubt, China's WTO entry will place unprecedented strains on the organization. The scale of what is involved in transforming China's economy and ensuring that it meets the promises it has made as part of the price of joining the WTO will place enormous claims on the WTO's small staff, which numbers just 200 or so professionals among a total of some 550 people.

In the West, there's a good deal of suspicion that China will be unwilling or unable to live up to its WTO agreements. That uncertainty is what drove negotiators to be so specific in detailing China's commitments. As a result, there is a far-reaching and unprecedented oversight process that will monitor China's compliance. An annual review of China's implementation of WTO agreements will take place for the first eight years of China's membership. This review is thorough. A total of 21 different WTO subsidiary bodies will be involved in reporting on implementation. These range from the Committee on Balance-of-Payments Restrictions to the Committee on Agriculture to the Committee on Rules of Origin. China will have to provide any information these committees request. Finally, after eight years of this sort of reporting, the WTO General Council will issue a final report during the tenth year following accession. These reviews will be extremely labor-intensive. The implicit assumption that China would be more or less left alone once it signed the WTO agreement is completely at odds with reality. Indeed, the problem could be quite different: the demands that China's entry will place on the WTO's staff could swamp the organization's capabilities.

On top of everything else, China has also asked for a good deal of technical assistance. Ideally, it would like hundreds of its government officials to receive training at WTO headquarters in Geneva soon after accession. China correctly perceives that the need for trade-related legal training is particularly acute. But the WTO doesn't have the resources to provide all the know-how that China requires. A simpler short-term expedient would be to train officials at universities in the US and Europe that have relevant courses. Another alternative would be to dramatically increase the WTO's technical resource capabilities. That could help other countries as well, but would take both time and money. This is one of a myriad of seemingly small issues that will have to be resolved if China is going to live up to its promises and be able to most fully realize the potential that WTO membership offers.

One of the most time-consuming issues for the WTO is the resolution of dumping cases. It's a highly contentious area that will become more important with China's entry into the trade body. Elaborate rules govern dumping, the practice of selling goods abroad for less than they cost to produce. Filing anti-dumping charges acts to slow down imports and often is used to protect uncompetitive local industries. China has been the largest target of anti-dumping charges in the past decade. A total of almost 350 cases were filed against it in the period from 1990 to 2000.

China is at a severe disadvantage in defending itself. For the purposes of dumping charges, the United States defines it as a non-market economy. Companies in most countries can defend themselves against anti-dumping charges by documenting their production costs. Chinese companies don't have this defense, which means that any prices Chinese companies charge can theoretically be challenged by an aggrieved competitor. As should be evident, China's is a mixed economy in which the state plays a strong role. But to call it a non-market economy is a stretch. China arguably has been the victim of heavy-handed politics as a result of the insistence by some of its negotiating partners that it be regarded as a non-market economy. The United States has long used this mechanism, although it wasn't explicitly recognized in law until China's WTO accession agreement. "We achieved a significant concession when we were able to gain China's agreement that we (and other WTO members) could continue to use this methodology for 15 years after China's accession to the WTO," noted USTR General Counsel Peter Davidson in testimony before the US Congress.[3] The problem with this method is that it means companies are subject to bureaucratic whims that allow the prosecuting country to use, for example, costs in India as a guide to what it cost to make a product in China. Investigations under these conditions are inherently political. Almost certainly, strains will only increase once China joins the WTO.

The US also won the right to use what it calls a "safeguard" mechanism to guard against rapid increases in exports of a particular product from China. Davidson said that this "significant concession" goes beyond what is generally allowed under WTO rules in two important ways. It allows, in Davidson's words, a "relatively lenient" standard, at least as seen from the perspective of the US. To bring dumping charges, an aggrieved party only has to show that the surge in imports from China causes "market disruption" (defined by the US Congress as "material injury") rather than the normal standard of "serious injury". Given that markets are constantly being disrupted by new competitors and more competitive products, this clause appears to be so broadly drawn as to allow virtually anyone hurt by a Chinese competitor to complain.

In another unprecedented clause, the WTO agreement also allows the US, or any other WTO member, to specifically target Chinese products in its complaints. Standard trade law doesn't permit this sort of discrimination. This defense will be available for 12 years after Chinese entry. Finally, the US won a specific clause aimed at textile and clothing exports from China. This permits the US to specifically target Chinese textile products even after the expiration of the existing textile restrictions (the Agreement on Textiles and Clothing) at the end of 2004. Instead, restrictions on Chinese clothing and textiles remain until the end of 2008.

MAKING TRADE SERVE DEVELOPMENT

The challenges China faces highlight some of the pressing issues confronting the WTO as it tries to live up to its mission of facilitating global prosperity. Nowhere are its challenges greater than in seeing that poor nations benefit from a more open trading order. Developing countries make up the majority of the WTO. Yet many of them cannot take advantage of the gains they could garner from more trade. Indeed, 23 of the least-developed countries have no representation in Geneva, although as many as 40 WTO meetings a week take place there.

Barriers to trade in goods and services need to be brought down, especially those that affect developing countries. Protectionism costs poor countries more than $100 billion annually, and probably more like $500 billion, annually.[4] The least-developed countries account for only 0.4% of world trade. They would benefit from greater openness, yet are hamstrung by rules that prevent them from enjoying the fruits of openness. For example, Vanuatu has been negotiating to join the WTO, but objections that it is unable to meet TRIPs standards have been raised by some large members and have stymied its entry. This sort of situation is untenable for an organization that prides itself on aiding trade and development. Moreover, additional technical assistance needs to be given so that these countries can capture more of the benefits of a liberal trade order. If they are victims rather than beneficiaries of the more liberal trading system, the merits of that system will be under even fiercer attack. If the WTO, with all its imperfections, doesn't succeed, rich countries will be even more dominant, or will make bilateral deals. There are a number of steps that could help the WTO become more effective in promoting trade for developing countries. A great deal has been written on trade and on development, and on the relationship between the two.[5] This isn't the place for an exhaustive treatment. But it's worth noting some of the most important points.

More International Policy Coherence: If we are to make globalization work better for developing countries, we need a more effective, open and accountable international system. We need global institutions to ensure that markets work for development. We know a lot about what needs to be done, but results have fallen far short of what they should be. An initiative known as the Integrated Framework was established in 1996 at the WTO's first ministerial conference in Singapore. Its aim was to analyze the effectiveness of trade-related technical assistance to the world's least-developed countries and to help integrate them into the world trading system.[6] Yet a recent review found that the Integrated Framework was flawed. An independent review in June 2000 highlighted problems that included a lack of priorities, weak administration and inadequate financial resources. The World Bank has now assumed leadership in the project. We have to see more concrete results from the endless studies and meetings that are conducted to examine globalization.

Cut Tariffs and Streamline Export Procedures: Total developing-country gains from a 50% cut in global tariffs would be around $150 billion — around three times as much as aid flows.[7] The $360 billion in agricultural subsidies that OECD member countries spend each year alone costs developing countries $20 billion in lost income. The Everything But Arms proposal, where all imports (except weapons) from least-developed countries enjoy duty-free access, is one approach worth studying. Another approach is the proposed Jubilee 2010 movement, which wants to target 2010 as the date for the removal of rich-country protectionism. Tariffs should be simplified. The paperwork involved in shipping goods and adhering to rigid product categories and rules of origin regulations could, and should, be minimized. With tariffs falling, paperwork shouldn't be mounting.

Special and Differential Treatment: There are numerous provisions for S&D treatment, but they haven't worked as well as intended. The standards are rather broad right now, covering simply the timing and size of tariff reductions that richer countries grant less-developed ones. But the treatment could be more nuanced. Can S&D be revised to have wider coverage? Can it allow for more exceptions? For example, it might be drawn to provide more assistance for single-commodity exporters and small economies. It might also allow for more favorable treatment for the production of vital drugs. We also need more workable country categories to take better account of different levels of development.

Political Will for Effective Policies: Developing countries must put rational economic and social policies in place. Development cannot occur without good governance. Effective governments are needed to build the legal, institutional and regulatory frameworks to put into effect market reforms. Education and basic health care aren't a luxury, but a prerequisite for growth. To compete in the global economy, developing countries need healthy and well-educated people, and greater access to knowledge, ideas, and new information and communication technologies. Trade and openness are necessary conditions for rapid growth. But they alone won't achieve the goal of development if they are built on a weak domestic base. One out of every five Africans lives in the midst of war or civil strife.[8] It's far-fetched to imagine that lasting economic development can occur in wartime.

Although trade must have a strong development component, we cannot turn the WTO into another development institution. There already exist a host of such institutions, such as the World Bank, regional development banks, the United Nations Development Project (UNDP), the United Nations International Development Organization (UNIDO) and the United Nations Conference on Trade and Development (UNCTAD). But the WTO can do much more to see that the potential of trade to help development is more fully realized.

At the same time, we mustn't blame poor economic performance on unfair policies by the rich world. Good economic performance must start with sensible domestic policies, ranging from good macroeconomic policy to fair and capable governmental institutions to sound corporate governance. Economist Jagdish Bhagwati has been a vocal proponent of free trade and has long criticized protectionism by rich countries. But he notes that poor countries generally have higher average tariff rates than rich countries and that anti-dumping actions by poor countries are starting to outnumber those by rich countries. Poor countries should improve their policies unilaterally, in trade and other areas, he says. "Even as we condemn rich-country protectionism, we must never forget to remind the poor countries that their own trade policies are often the cause of their dismal performance," writes Bhagwati. "Just contrast the splendid export performance of the East Asian economies ... with the abysmal export performance of India for nearly 40 years. Both groups of countries faced virtually the same trade barriers abroad."[9]

TRADE, LABOR AND THE ENVIRONMENT

The WTO must focus on trade. But it does have a role in facilitating progress on other issues. After all, the WTO charter tasks the group with "raising standards of living, *ensuring full employment* and a large and steadily growing volume of real income and effective demand, and expanding the production of and trade in goods and services ... in a manner consistent with [member countries'] respective needs and concerns at different levels of economic development".[10]

With articulate and well-organized critics leading the charge against free trade, it's going to be increasingly difficult for trade negotiators and political leaders to simply ignore the call for a more immediate pay-off between trade and adherence to internationally recognized labor rights. Liberal trade advocates need to shift the terms of the debate by showing how trade can create employment. Once the pay-off in employment generated by trade is better understood, the rights of workers and the labor standards that have been adopted by the ILO can be discussed more fruitfully. As matters stand now, more work is being done on trade and labor standards than on trade and employment.

World leaders should convene a ministerial meeting on trade and employment, outside of the auspices of the WTO. Such a meeting could be arranged by the ILO, UNCTAD or the UN Economic and Social Committee, although the WTO could participate for the sake of policy coherence and to ensure that the linkages between trade and employment were represented. If such a meeting were held by the WTO, many countries wouldn't participate, for fear that they were committing themselves to a link between labor standards and trade. The meeting should be at a high political level because we need political guidance as to how we can make trade work for the creation of employment. It should be a one-time meeting, to avoid giving the impression that we are setting up a permanent body, and it should ask other competent authorities to continue work on the issue. The result of such a high-level meeting could be the creation of a commission on employment that can have leaders of responsible international organizations as members to discuss related aspects of trade, employment and labor rights. The meeting would provide a forum for developing countries to explain how they think trade could help them to create new jobs by, for instance, diversifying their economies away from the export of a single commodity, such as cocoa or coffee. But in any case, trade linkages shouldn't be part of the solution.

We should also examine how far industrialized and developing countries have benefited from the increase in world trade. Has the right kind of investment gone to developing countries? Has trade helped them to create enough jobs?

We also need to discuss the relationship between economic and trade performance and the observance of labor rights in general and core labor rights in particular. It may be that the enforcement of labor rights has positive economic benefits for advanced countries, but less-certain consequences in developing countries.

For advanced economies, however, the economic benefits may not be due just to the observance of labor rights but to other factors, such as the introduction of new technology that enhances skills. Skill enhancement, of course, can be facilitated because labor standards and core labor rights are being observed.

We also need to investigate seriously the claims that if labor standards aren't internationally supervised, there may be a "race to the bottom", in which countries seek to compete by lowering their standards in general. We still need to determine, however, whether there is, in fact, a race to the bottom with regard to wages and core labor rights. We should examine the widening wage gap in many developing countries to determine whether it's due to trade liberalization or to the wrong domestic policies. We should consider whether trade policies can be managed in a way that would narrow the gap.

The WTO alone cannot work to promote the cause of free trade and development. If trade is to be harnessed to the development process, the WTO must work with other international institutions. Some obvious candidates to work with on these broader issues are UNCTAD, UNIDO, the UNDP, the World Bank and the IMF. We also need to have more involvement in development programs — "buy-in" and "ownership" in the current jargon — by the recipient countries, so that countries can use trade-related programs more effectively to further their development goals.

At some point in the future, we may need to establish a UN-sponsored council on employment, or a world council on employment, that would permanently coordinate trade and employment policies and focus international attention on these vital issues. If we can agree that trade helps to create jobs, particularly in developing countries, then we won't need to go around and convince people to join a new round of trade talks. If trade has no positive impact on jobs, however, we should construct a different kind of round to meet the requirements of developing countries. As far as the developing world is concerned, the primary goal for trade is to create jobs. If we can address this goal in the new round, then we can look forward to a development round with appropriate substance rather than mere semantics.

Activists have also seized on the environmental degradation often associated with economic growth as another reason to slow down trade liberalization. The WTO can play a role by working to end harmful subsidies that both distort trade and harm the environment. There are many examples of these in the agriculture, fishery and energy sectors. For example, the World Wide Fund for Nature (WWF) calculates that Argentinian fisheries policies during the 1990s ended up costing the economy about $500 million. A best-practices set of policies would have had a net benefit of about $5.1 billion. In Tanzania, the WWF figures that $80 million in benefits from timber exports was matched by an equal amount of environmental degradation.[11] Some WTO member countries have proposed ending subsidies that lead to industrial overcapacity and also harm the environment. A new round of trade talks could spur greater global adoption of environmentally friendly technologies by lowering trade barriers.

As with labor issues, injecting environmental concerns into trade negotiations adds another layer of complexity to what are already politically difficult and technically complex issues. The aim of the WTO is to deal with trade and only with trade. More suitable means must be found to deal with the environment. The United Nations Environmental Program is better equipped to take primary responsibility. It can work with the WTO's Committee on Trade and Environment. But it would be preferable to have a global organization with the same stature as the WTO. The best solution might be to set up a World Environment Organization, which has the legal status to deal with the enforcement of environmental standards.

Moreover, a closer look at the facts should allay many of the environmental concerns associated with increased trade. There are some empirical studies suggesting that pollution increases in the early stages of development but decreases after a certain income level has been reached.[12] Given that some of the worst environmental degradation occurs among the poorest of the poor — people who are largely outside the market economy, let alone the global economy — freer trade should raise their living standards and eventually slow down or reverse environmental deterioration. Trade-restrictive practices, be they through outright protectionism or through trade sanctions, can only result in more impoverishment and thus increased environmental degradation. Expanding trade volume doesn't automatically cure environmental ills, but at least it offers the opportunity for improved living conditions and, thus, enhanced environmental quality.

REFORMING THE WTO TO HELP THE POOR

One of the key sparks for both world wars was economic discrimination and trade warfare. Although GATT was envisioned only as a stopgap organization until a binding international trade body could be established, it nonetheless proved quite effective. During seven rounds of GATT negotiations, tariffs on manufactured goods were sliced from an average of 40% in 1948 to about 6% in 1980 and just 4% now. But the issues have now moved beyond the relatively straightforward task of lowering tariffs to encompass various other measures used to restrict trade. Quotas and anti-dumping suits, both wielded largely by developed countries, have become a new way to restrict trade. There is a great deal that needs to be done, and can be done, to see that the WTO functions more effectively.

We need to show the developing world that new trade talks will guarantee concrete benefits for the less-developed countries. The agenda for the developed countries has been quite well established, whether in dealing with agriculture, industry and services or broader areas such as intellectual-property rights, environmental standards, investment regimes, competition policies and anti-dumping procedures. It's time now for developing countries to stand up. For the first time, developing countries are likely to spend more time pushing a positive agenda in the next round of trade negotiations than on blocking proposals for liberalization from developed countries. Here are some of the key items on the developing-world's agenda.[13]

There is general agreement that tariff- and quota-free market access for the 49 least-developed countries is a sensible policy. These countries are, by definition, outside the mainstream of the world economy and have little trade or foreign investment. Bringing these countries into the world economy, and seeing that they share some of its benefits, represents a key challenge for the WTO. In 1996, the WTO decided on an action plan that promised to push for free access for exports from these countries. The results have been disappointing. For example, as of 2000, only about 20% of exports from the least-developed countries to the US were duty free. However, in 2001 the European Union introduced the EBA (Everything But Arms) policy that in principle will allow full access for products from the least-developed countries in the future. This is an interesting plan in spite of the fact that important products such as rice, bananas and sugar aren't included in the initial phase. Indeed, agricultural exporting countries have, cynically, termed it the "everything-but-farms initiative". However, Jagdish Bhagwati worries that, by drawing a line between poor countries, it could hurt countries that are just above the line. Preferences can also send a message to poor countries that they can only compete with the help of special assistance. "It is surely better to dismantle protection on labor-intensive products altogether and to direct special and generous aid and technical assistance programs to the least-developed countries instead."[14]

Second, there should be more flexibility in the implementation of WTO-mandated standards, particularly the landmark TRIPs intellectual-property rights measures. Although developing and less-developed countries have longer periods of time in which to phase in these standards, implementation will be difficult nonetheless. As it is now, stiff penalties can be imposed for implementation failures, even for countries that don't have the institutional ability to put these WTO requirements into place.

Third, developed countries need to implement the principle of special and differential treatment more fully. Developing countries need a handicap, just as if they were playing golf. Although WTO agreements call for countries to take the development situation in a country into account, these measures aren't binding and in many areas there has been no serious implementation. Freer movement of labor from developing to developed countries is an obvious area of interest where there has been little serious negotiation.

Fourth, anti-dumping procedures should be amended so that they aren't used as a guise for protectionism, a practice that usually victimizes developing countries. An analysis of anti-dumping investigations from 1995 to 1997 showed that six of the top 10 countries under investigation for new anti-dumping measures were developing countries. Five were from Asia. Dumping investigations against Korea jumped following the onset of the financial crisis, although Korea's competitiveness genuinely was heightened by a weak currency. China's entry will make reform of the anti-dumping system even more urgent.

Fifth, there must be no linkage between trade and social issues. Developing countries cannot accept such a linkage. It's extremely unlikely that such a linkage would be the best way of improving labor standards. Trade agreements are so complex that adding a highly political element will add an unnecessary burden to what is already a difficult process.

Sixth, we should push for an earlier liberalization of the Agreement on Clothing and Textiles, the restrictive covenant governing the textile and garment trade, perhaps in 2003 rather than at the end of 2004. At the very least, the phase-out should be speeded up and implemented in a way that shows good faith on the part of the rich world. While developing countries usually have to implement promised reforms immediately, developed countries won a 10-year phase-out period for textiles. Liberalization is being implemented only haltingly; much more could be done in a way that shows a political commitment to free trade.

Besides this agenda, there are a number of other measures that could make the WTO itself more effective.

Facilitating Accession: Accession procedures shouldn't take so long. If the WTO is going to be a truly global trade organization, there cannot be the sense that existing members use the accession process to squeeze the last drop of blood out of applicant countries. It should be enough for newcomers to simply adopt all existing commitments that current members have accepted. China has been negotiating on and off for more than 15 years. The 19 least-developed countries waiting for accession account for less than 0.2% of world trade, so their entry would be unlikely to disrupt the WTO.[15] They should be allowed to join with a minimum of conditions. Another solution could be some sort of transitional period for membership, a kind of probation or associate status. (See the following section for a fuller discussion of this subject.)

Streamlining Consensus-based Decision Making: Running an organization as complex as the WTO on the basis of consensus is no longer practical. We must investigate alternatives. The World Bank and the IMF offer possible models. The World Bank has a Development Committee and the IMF has an Interim Committee. These committees discuss and decide basic policy issues. British Prime Minister Tony Blair has suggested empowering a group of eminent persons that would help speed up WTO decisions. This body would narrow down the number of decisions on which the entire membership decides. Another idea would be some sort of council with rotating membership that is tasked with building consensus and narrowing differences on major and controversial issues. Such a group could assist the General Council in making the consensus-based decision-making process more efficient.

Improving the Green Room Process: Developing countries understandably don't like the fact that they are excluded from many of the most sensitive negotiations, which take place in the Director-general's so-called Green Room, a room with fading green paint adjacent to his office. The room is physically small, limiting the number of participants. This physical restriction has led members to complain that they are being excluded from important informal meetings. A closed-circuit television link or other real-time communication method to include outside participants would go a long way toward overcoming the suspicions of countries that are kept out of the Green Room proceedings. Full communication between the Green Room participants and the General Council must be maintained at all times.

Reforming the Dispute Settlement Body: The backbone of the WTO, and what sets it apart from GATT, is the Dispute Settlement Body, which handles trade conflicts between member countries. The number of trade disputes has multiplied in recent years, putting a strain on the panels. Enforcement of the panels' rulings is still lax, rendering the chance for nations to procrastinate. Member countries are becoming more wary of the panels' rulings, especially when they represent interpretations of unclear WTO rules. Rulings on environment-related legislation that involves trade remain especially contentious.

Improving Internal and External Transparency: To promote internal transparency, documents need to be de-classified and redistributed more quickly. Although there have been reforms in this area, there's still room for further improvement. External transparency is a more complex issue. To build international support, the WTO should reach out to non-governmental organizations and others with an interest in trade issues. NGOs cannot have a place at the negotiating table and they cannot be part of the dispute-settlement process. Because they aren't elected representatives, they need to work through their own governments. But the WTO should seek a method to ensure that it hears their concerns. The simplest solution would be to apply the United Nations accreditation system that gives NGOs a forum for a more formal exchange of views.

Increasing Technical Assistance: Many developing countries don't have adequate laws. They don't have trained lawyers. They are scrambling to stay afloat in the face of high unemployment and other problems. The WTO is typically not a high priority for these hard-pressed countries, but it's important that the organization does more to help members with limited institutional capabilities. Some members have jointly established a legal advisory center specifically to assist the least-developed countries and developing countries. But the WTO itself must do much more, if members are going to be able to take advantage of the opportunities freer trade presents — and if they are going to be able to meet their WTO commitments. The need for technical assistance is acute in some of the complex new TRIPs and TRIMs measures.

REFORMING WTO ENTRY PROCEDURES

In many ways, the WTO has been a phenomenal success. When the GATT was founded in 1947, fewer than two dozen countries signed on. At the time the WTO came into being, in 1995, there were only about 100 members. Today there are 142 and, with the more than two dozen in line to join, virtually every one of the world's traders is either in the organization or would like to join it. Only a few outliers such as North Korea are not in the WTO or trying to join. WTO members now account for more than 95% of world trade.

Yet as China's experience shows, the current accession process doesn't work as well as it should. There is simply too long a lag between the time accession procedures begin and when it occurs. Moreover, there's a belief among applicant countries that the goalposts keep being moved as negotiations drag on and domestic interests in member countries raise new issues.

With about 30 nations queuing up to join, a way must be found to expedite the process, to get countries more quickly enjoying the rights and fulfilling the responsibilities of the WTO. This is especially important given that some major nations still haven't joined. Applications from Russia, Saudi Arabia, Vietnam and Iran are all pending. It would be far better for the world trading system to be more inclusive, to bring applicants at least into the anteroom of the world trading organization, if not immediately into the main hall. Indeed, China's struggle to join the WTO points to a larger issue: how can the trade body accelerate entry procedures to enable those who want to join to be admitted more quickly and yet still maintain its integrity as a strong, rules-based organization?

It's proper that standards are maintained and the rules that bind the organization aren't diluted. Yet, for the sake of making the WTO as inclusive as possible, it's important that the entry process be accelerated, especially now that nations that account for the bulk of the world's trade are in the WTO tent. Of course, there's a tension between the need to get more countries into the trade organization and the need to maintain its integrity.

As matters stand now, though, it's apparent that the system isn't working quickly enough to pull them into the WTO. That's particularly true for so-called transition economies, which are in the midst of moving from socialism to the market. The former planned economies are forced to make a double adjustment. They must shift from a centrally driven command economy to a market-led one. And they must make the change from an autocratic economy to one that is governed by international rules. Most notably in this category, Russia is now negotiating WTO accession. The world shouldn't wait another decade or more to bring Russia into the WTO fold. The world's least-developed countries should also be encouraged to join. Thirty of the 49 countries that fall into this category are already WTO members. The others should be brought into the organization in some fashion as soon as possible, so that they can learn about and benefit from the world trading order.

For these economies, at least, there should be a transitional stage of WTO membership. One model to examine would be an associate membership category, much like the European Union has. Associate members could take part in non-binding meetings but only observe at binding meetings. Countries would be initiated or acculturated into the WTO in a process that would be akin to an apprenticeship. They would have the opportunity to be judged and the time to make the transition.

The problem with the existing system is that it gives a tremendous degree of power to any individual member of the club. In the case of China, even after the European Union and the United States had come to agreement, Mexico's inability to reach a bilateral accord with China alone could have been enough to stop Beijing's bid. (Instead, Mexico promised that it wouldn't hold up Beijing's accession. In the end, the two sides struck a bilateral agreement the week before the WTO's working party on China approved the accession agreement.) Issues or trading relationships that are relatively small, in an overall sense, can hold up trade talks. In some respects, the WTO is run like the membership of an exclusive club, where any member can blackball a prospective applicant. There are good reasons why the system developed the way that it did and, while it does include important safeguards, it may not be the best way to move forward.

Contrast these cumbersome entry procedures with membership in the World Bank and the IMF. China applied to these organizations in 1980 and joined that same year. There are, of course, vast differences between the cases, because membership in the World Bank and the IMF doesn't carry the same sort of legally binding commitments that membership of the WTO does. Still, GATT wasn't legally binding, yet China was unable to join. The long delay is a reminder that the WTO could reform its procedures.

QUESTIONS FOR THE WTO'S FUTURE

The WTO is one of the cornerstones of growth in a world that has seen more economic progress in the past half-century than at any time in human history. China's entry into the WTO is a crowning achievement, both in terms of China's own economic development and the WTO's legitimacy. But the WTO cannot stand still. There is much that can be done to ensure that the development process evolves more quickly. Misguided though many of the protests against globalization are, many critics have pointed out flaws that should be corrected if trade is to serve as a means to the end of a richer, freer world, one where more people have more choices about how they want to lead their lives. It would be a tragedy if the hard-won gains of a more liberal trading order were squandered. But it would also be tragic if China and the world don't fully seize the opportunities presented by globalization to ensure that trade and growth benefit those who need it most.

WTO Entry: How can we simplify the complex procedures for the low-income countries which don't have much to offer as an entry fee? Can we devise some other means to get non-members involved, such as some form of associate membership, in order to prepare them for formal accession?

Internal and External Transparency: Given the frustrations of some smaller countries, which feel that they are left out of key discussions, can informal consultative groups of member countries be devised as a way of improving internal communications? Would the WTO process be improved or impaired by having a regular exchange of opinions through some advisory forums of representatives from civil society that would include not only NGOs from rich countries but also those from developing countries and members of the corporate world?

Clarification and Review of Rules: How can we clarify trade rules when they clash with other agreements, such as Multilateral Environmental Agreements, so that trade conflicts can be prevented and trade isn't restricted? Can anti-dumping procedures be amended so that they are used only as a protection against genuine dumping practices and not as a means to restrict competition?

Policy Coherence: How can we make trade more consistent with development? Can we set up committees of heads of international organizations to work together on specific issues such as globalization or employment? Can the Integrated Framework be reformed so that it works more effectively?

Sustainable Development: How can trade help eradicate poverty and, at the same time, be environmentally benign and consistent with social goals?

These are big issues, ones that are easy to ignore in a world that is involved with the details of drafting and implementing detailed rules. But the WTO and its members ignore these issues at their peril.

ક્ર   ક્ર   ક્ર

One of the reasons for the backlash against globalization is the loss of sovereignty over some economic policies among countries. This is a fact we need to understand. We need to develop sensible policies as a way of responding to these sentiments. But we cannot ignore the need for governments to reform themselves. Governments can, and should, play a significant role in building and supporting legal and other institutions to promote and support efficient markets. There is a need for governments to be both more prepared in building a market-friendly environment and simultaneously less interventionist in the market itself. Governments need to provide a good macroeconomic framework. They have to play the role of referee in banking systems and in the markets at large. This isn't a role for the WTO. But any agenda for freer trade must be mindful of this need to build stronger institutions throughout societies.

At the WTO, the poorer countries must have their agenda represented. This is both good economic sense and good political sense. Otherwise, there is likely to be increased polarization between the developed and the developing world. For example, a meeting of the 49 least-developed countries held in Zanzibar, Tanzania, in July 2001, called for opposition to a new trade round or, indeed, any further trade liberalization unless the rich world reformed agricultural trade. There can be other trade-offs. If the developed world wants to discuss, say, intellectual-property rights, then the developing world should negotiate a wide-ranging discussion of the anti-dumping regime, which is often used to keep goods out of wealthier countries. If the developed world wants to talk about information-technology products, the developing world could ask for talks on accelerating the phase-out of the restrictions on textiles, the Agreement on Textiles and Clothing. If the developed world wants to discuss industrial tariffs, the developing world could push for talks on market access for agricultural products. The needs of the poor must be represented. Basic humanitarian needs such as access to cheap medicines must be met. The landmark agreement in mid-2001 between the South African government and major pharmaceutical companies to provide a cocktail of inexpensive anti-AIDs drugs marks a pivotal moment in leading toward a new order.

So far, liberalization commitments by richer countries have often only been implemented half-heartedly. Developed countries have back-loaded their commitments, saving most of the gains for the years just before the deadline expires. This is clearly the case with textiles and apparel. World trade in agricultural goods continues to be distorted by all manner of provisions such as export subsidies, domestic support schemes, tariff peaks and tariff escalations. New barriers in the form of sanitary and phytosanitary standards, which slow exports and imports of food, have appeared. While some of these represent legitimate concerns, others are clearly trade barriers. Developing countries need the institutional capacity to help take advantage of developed markets, especially when faced with complex and often cumbersome sanitary and technical requirements.

The role of China will be key. China typically hasn't taken a leading role in most international organizations. Will it push for a developing-world agenda, perhaps by teaming up with other major developing nations such as India and Brazil? Initial, informal discussions reveal a desire by China to play a significant role in the WTO. In the long run, China's most appropriate role may be as a bridge between the developed and developing member countries, given the dual role it plays as a developing economy and an emerging superpower. More immediately, because China will have a voice in any new trade round, its accession could help shift the balance of power in upcoming trade talks more in favor of developing nations.

The stakes are higher than they have ever been. China's entry into the WTO can signal an age of increased world trade and the greater prosperity and security that accompany it. The terror attacks on the World Trade Center were meant to strike at the heart of the liberal, open order which the WTO works to extend. A fitting memorial to the more than 2500 people from about 80 nations who died on September 11, 2001 would be an ever-more open trading order, one that gave more people in more countries more choices than they have had before.

---

[1]   This section is drawn from Chapter 1 ("The Challenge of Globalisation") in *Eliminating World Poverty: Making Globalisation Work for the Poor, White Paper on International Development, Presented to Parliament by the Secretary of State for International Development*, London, The Stationery Office, 2000.

[2]   Elena Ianchovichina, Will Martin and Emiko Fukase, *Assessing the Implications of Merchandise Trade Liberalization in China's Accession to WTO*, Washington, D.C., World Bank, 2000, pp. 30–31 (mimeo).

[3]   The testimony was on August 2, 2001, before the US-China Security Review Commission. It was reprinted as "USTR Counsel on China's 'Imminent' WTO Accession" in the American Chamber of Commerce (Hong Kong) *Amcham Bulletin*, August 2001.

[4]   This is an unpublished estimate from the World Bank, dated March 2001. One study that the Bank cites says that developing countries would gain $455 billion annually from full merchandise liberalization alone; it notes that the impact from full services liberalization would likely be even greater.

[5]   *Eliminating World Poverty, op.cit.*, is one of the best current documents that represents a synthesized consensus view of what should be done.

[6]   The institutions involved are the WTO, UNCTAD, ITC (International Trade Center), UNDP, IMF and the World Bank.

[7] This figure is quoted in *Eliminating World Poverty, op.cit.,* p. 69. Much of this section is drawn from the ensuing discussion in the White Paper.

[8] James D. Wolfensohn, "Putting Africa Front and Center", July 16, 2001, at www.worldbank.org/html/extdr/extme/jdwsp071601.htm.

[9] Jagdish Bhagwati, "Targeting Rich-Country Protectionism", *Finance & Development*, September 2001.

[10] *Agreement Establishing the World Trade Organization*, April 15, 1994. Downloaded from www.wto.org.

[11] World Wide Fund for Nature, *How Can Multilateral Trade Deliver Sustainable Development Outcomes?*, Brussels, WWF European Policy Office, 2001, p. 3.

[12] Supachai Panitchpakdi, *Globalization and Trade in the New Millennium*, Bangkok, Ministry of Commerce, 2001, p. 257.

[13] This section relies heavily on the discussion in the Economic and Social Commission for Asia and the Pacific (ESCAP), *Development Through Globalization and Partnership in the Twenty-First Century*, New York, N.Y., United Nations, 2000, especially pp. 59–96.

[14] Bhagwati, *op.cit.*

[15] ESCAP, *op.cit.*, p. 88.

Appendices

Appendix 1: Summary of US–China Bilateral WTO Agreement, February 2, 2000

AGRICULTURE

The Agreement would eliminate barriers and increase access for US exports across a broad range of commodities. Commitments include:

- Significant cuts in tariffs that will be completed by January 2004. Overall average for agricultural products will be 17.5% and for US priority products 14% (down from 31%).
- Establishment of a tariff-rate quota [TRQ] system for imports of bulk commodities, e.g., wheat, corn, cotton, barley, and rice, that provides a share of the TRQ for private traders. Specific rules on how the TRQ will operate and increased transparency in the process will help ensure that imports occur. Significant and growing quota quantities subject to tariffs that average between 1–3%.
- Immediate elimination of the tariff-rate quota system for barley, peanut oil, sunflower-seed oil, cottonseed oil, and a phase-out for soybean oil.

- The right to import and distribute products without going through a state-trading enterprise or middleman.
- Elimination of export subsidies on agricultural products. China has also agreed to the elimination of Sanitary and Phytosanitary Standards (SPS) barriers that are not based on scientific evidence.

INDUSTRIAL PRODUCTS

China would lower tariffs and eliminate broad systemic barriers to US exports, such as limits on who can import goods and distribute them in China, as well as barriers such as quotas and licenses on US products.

TARIFFS
- Tariffs cut from an average of 24.6% to an average of 9.4% overall and 7.1% on US priority products.
- China will participate in the Information Technology Agreement (ITA) and eliminate all tariffs on products such as computers, telecommunications equipment, semiconductors, computer equipment, and other high-technology products.
- In the auto sector, China will cut tariffs from the current 80–100% level to 25% by mid-2006, with the largest cuts in the first years after accession.
- Auto parts tariffs will be cut to an average of 10% by mid-2006.
- In the wood and paper sectors, tariffs will drop from present levels of 12–18% on wood and 15–25% on paper down to levels generally between 5% and 7.5%.

    China will also be implementing the vast majority of the chemical harmonization initiative. Under that initiative, tariffs will be at 0, 5.5 and 6.5% for products in each category.

ELIMINATION OF QUOTAS AND LICENSES

WTO rules bar quotas and other quantitative restrictions. China has agreed to eliminate these restrictions with phase-ins limited to five years.

- China will eliminate existing quotas upon accession for the top US priorities (e.g. fiber optic cable). It will phase out remaining quotas, generally by 2002, but no later than 2005.
- Quotas will grow from current trade levels at a 15% annual rate in order to ensure that market access increases progressively.
- Auto quotas will be phased out by 2005. In the interim, the base-level quota will be $6 billion (the level prior to China's auto industrial policy), and this will grow by 15% annually until elimination.

RIGHT TO IMPORT AND DISTRIBUTE

Trading rights and distribution are among the top concerns for US manufacturers and agricultural exporters. At present, China severely restricts trading rights (the right to import and export) and the ability to own and operate distribution networks. Under the Agreement, trading rights and distribution services will be progressively phased in over three years. China will also open up sectors related to distribution services, such as repair and maintenance, warehousing, trucking and air courier services.

SERVICES

China has made commitments to phase out most restrictions in a broad range of services sectors, including distribution, banking, insurance, telecommunications, professional services such as accountancy and legal consulting, business and computer related services, motion pictures and video and sound recording services. China will also participate in the Basic Telecommunications and Financial Services Agreements.

GRANDFATHERING
China will grandfather the existing level of market access already in effect at the time of China's accession for US services companies currently operating in China. This will protect existing American businesses operating under contractual or shareholder agreements or a license from new restrictions as China phases in their commitments. [This means than any benefits companies currently enjoy will remain in effect.]

DISTRIBUTION AND RELATED SERVICES
China generally prohibits foreign firms from distributing products other than those they make in China, or from controlling their own distribution networks. Under the Agreement, China has agreed to liberalize wholesaling and retailing services for most products, including imported goods, throughout China in three years. In addition, China has agreed to open up the logistical chain of related services such as maintenance and repair, storage and warehousing, packaging, advertising, trucking and air express services, marketing, and customer support in three to four years.

TELECOMMUNICATIONS
China now prohibits foreign investment in telecom-munications services. For the first time, China has agreed to permit direct investment in telecommunications businesses. China will also participate in the Basic Telecommunications

Agreement. Specific commitments include:

- Regulatory Principles: China has agreed to implement the pro-competitive regulatory principles embodied in the Basic Telecommunications Agreement (including interconnection rights and independent regulatory authority) and will allow foreign suppliers to use any technology they choose to provide telecommunications services.
- China will gradually phase out all geographic restrictions for paging and value-added services in two years, mobile voice and data services in five years, and domestic and international services in six years.
- China will permit 50% foreign equity share for value-added and paging services two years after accession, 49% foreign equity share for mobile voice and data services five years after accession, and for domestic and international services six years after accession.

INSURANCE

Currently, only two US insurers have access to China's market. Under the agreement:

- China agreed to award licenses solely on the basis of prudential criteria, with no economic-needs test or quantitative limits on the number of licenses issued.
- China will progressively eliminate all geographic limitations within three years. Internal branching will be permitted consistent with the elimination of these restrictions.
- China will expand the scope of activities for foreign insurers to include group, health and pension lines of insurance, phased in over five years. Foreign property and casualty firms will be able to insure large-scale

commercial risks nationwide immediately upon accession.

- China agreed to allow 50% ownership for life insurance. Life insurers may also choose their own joint-venture partners. For non-life, China will allow branching or 51% ownership on accession and wholly owned subsidiaries in two years. Reinsurance is completely open upon accession (100%, no restrictions).

BANKING

Currently foreign banks are not permitted to do local currency business with Chinese clients (a few can engage in local currency business with their foreign clients). China imposes severe geographic restrictions on the establishment of foreign banks.

- China has committed to full market access in five years for US banks.
- Foreign banks will be able to conduct local currency business with Chinese enterprises starting two years after accession.
- Foreign banks will be able to conduct local currency business with Chinese individuals from five years after accession.
- Foreign banks will have the same rights (national treatment) as Chinese banks within designated geographic areas.
- Both geographic and customer restrictions will be removed in five years.
- Non-bank financial companies can offer auto financing upon accession.

SECURITIES

China will permit minority foreign-owned joint ventures to engage in fund management on the same terms as Chinese firms. By three years after accession, foreign ownership of these joint ventures will be allowed to rise to 49%. As the scope of business expands for Chinese firms, foreign joint-venture securities companies will enjoy the same expansion in scope of business. In addition, 33% foreign-owned joint ventures will be allowed to underwrite domestic equity issues and underwrite and trade in international equity and all corporate and government debt issues.

PROFESSIONAL SERVICES

China has made strong commitments regarding professional services, including the areas of law, accounting, management consulting, tax consulting, architecture, engineering, urban planning, medical and dental services, and computer and related services. China's commitments will lead to greater market access opportunities and increased certainty for American companies doing business in China.

MOTION PICTURES, VIDEOS, SOUND RECORDINGS

China will allow the 20 films to be imported on a revenue-sharing basis in each of the three years after accession. US firms can form joint ventures to distribute videos, software entertainment, and sound recordings and to own and operate cinemas.

PROTOCOL PROVISIONS

Commitments in China's WTO Protocol and Working Party Report establish rights and obligations enforceable through WTO dispute-settlement procedures. We have agreed on key provisions relating to antidumping and subsidies, protection against import surges, technology-transfer requirements, and offsets, as well as practices of state-owned and state-invested enterprises. These rules are of special importance to US workers and business.

China has agreed to implement the TRIMs Agreement upon accession, eliminate and cease enforcing trade and foreign exchange balancing requirements, as well as local content requirements, refuse to enforce contracts imposing these requirements, and only impose or enforce laws or other provisions relating to the transfer of technology or other know-how if they are in accordance with the WTO agreements on protection of intellectual-property rights and trade-related investment measures.

These provisions will also help protect American firms against forced technology transfers. China has agreed that, upon accession, it will not condition investment approvals, import licenses, or any other import approval process on performance requirements of any kind, including: local content requirements, offsets, transfer of technology, or requirements to conduct research and development in China.

ANTIDUMPING AND SUBSIDIES METHODOLOGY

The agreed protocol provisions ensure that American firms and workers will have strong protection against unfair trade practices including dumping and subsidies. The US and China have agreed that we will be able to maintain our current antidumping methodology (treating China as a non-market economy) in future antidumping cases.

This provision will remain in force for 15 years after China's accession to the WTO. Moreover, when we apply our countervailing duty law to China we will be able to take the special characteristics of China's economy into account when we identify and measure any subsidy benefit that may exist.

PRODUCT-SPECIFIC SAFEGUARD

The agreed provisions for the protocol package also ensure that American domestic firms and workers will have strong protection against rapid increases of imports.

To do this, the Product-Specific Safeguard provision sets up a special mechanism to address increased imports that cause or threaten to cause market disruption to a US industry. This mechanism, which is in addition to other WTO Safeguards provisions, differs from traditional safeguard measures. It permits the United States to address imports solely from China, rather than from the whole world, that are a significant cause of material injury through measures such as import restrictions. Moreover, the United States will be able to apply restraints unilaterally based on legal standards that differ from those in the WTO Safeguards Agreement. This could permit action in more cases. The Product-Specific Safeguard will remain in force for 12 years after China accedes to the WTO.

STATE-OWNED AND STATE-INVESTED ENTERPRISES

The Protocol addresses important issues related to the Chinese government's involvement in the economy. China has agreed that it will ensure that state-owned and state-invested enterprises will make purchases and sales based solely on commercial considerations, such as price, quality, availability and marketability, and that it will provide US firms with the opportunity to compete for sales and purchases on non-discriminatory terms and conditions.

China has also agreed that it will not influence these commercial decisions (either directly or indirectly) except in a WTO-consistent manner. With respect to applying WTO rules to state-owned and state-invested enterprises, we have clarified in several ways that these firms are subject to WTO disciplines:

- Purchases of goods or services by these state-owned and state-invested enterprises do not constitute "government procurement" and thus are subject to WTO rules.

- We have clarified the status of state-owned and state-invested enterprises under the WTO Agreement on Subsidies and Countervailing Measures. This will help ensure that we can effectively apply our trade law to these enterprises when it is appropriate to do so.

TEXTILES

China's protocol package will include a provision drawn from our 1997 bilateral textiles agreement, which permits US companies and workers to respond to increased imports of textile and apparel products. This textile safeguard will remain in effect until December 31, 2008, which is four years after the WTO Agreement on Textiles and Clothing expires.

Appendix 2: The Sino-EU Agreement on China's Accession to the WTO: Results of the Bilateral Negotiations

The following is an overview of the results achieved by the EU in addition to the Sino-US accord. Some of the issues covered did not form part of that agreement, while others had already been the subject of negotiations between China and other partners, but have been further improved by the EU. In both cases, the list below is confined to commitments which were secured explicitly by the European Union.

INDUSTRIAL GOODS

IMPORT TARIFFS

As for specific EU priorities not covered by China's previous bilateral agreements, these were concentrated on 150 specific products varying from gin to building materials. On these EU-specific priorities, an additional reduction of 40% on top of earlier offers was obtained (the tariff average falling from 18.6% to 10.6%). Tariffs on all spirits will be aligned to a level of 10%. There will be no difference in the treatment of whiskey, cognac, gin, etc. The presently applied tariff level is still at 65%. Tariffs on key cosmetics products will come down to a level of 10% (currently up to 30%). This implies good prospects for a sector which already exports up to EU 7 billion worldwide.

On leather and leather articles, negotiations focused on 13 specific products which account for 60% of total EU exports in this sector. China agreed a reduction on these products from 20–25% to 10%.

On textiles, China made some further improvements to the previous offer. China's textiles tariffs are very close to the levels of the EU and far lower than almost all other textile-exporting countries.

Tariffs on five particular footwear products which account for more than 70% of EU footwear exports will be reduced from 25% to 10%.

Marble/building stones are popular articles in China's enormous construction market. On the five most important products, tariffs will also be reduced from 25% to 10%. On ceramics, China agreed to reduce tariffs on 11 key products from 24.5–35% to 10–15%. And tariffs on six particular glass products will be reduced from 24.5% to 5%.

On 52 particular products in the important machinery and appliances sector, which accounts for 26% of total EU exports, tariffs will be cut to 5–10% from levels up to 35%.

• Quotas: China's quota on Europe's fertilizer exports will be liberalized upon accession, and restrictions in place this year will be immediately relaxed.

• State Trading: Liberalization of import monopolies on oil and fertilizer — China has agreed to open the crude- and processed-oil sectors, as well as fertilizer, to private traders through a process of gradual liberalization. This means that firms will no longer be obliged to go exclusively through China's state importers when shipping oil and fertilizer to China. These sectors are the most significant domains where a state import monopoly has been in place.

Liberalization of export monopoly on silk — EU firms will be able to buy raw silk directly from Chinese producers (who make 70% of the world total). Until now all purchases had to go through state export channels. This will bring substantial benefits to the EU's numerous manufacturers of ties, scarves and other high-value silk garments and accessories.

- Motor Vehicles: The EU and China agreed on a range of improvements for EU firms which produce cars, vans and trucks in China. For those who have invested in joint-venture manufacturing operations (or will do so in the future), there are three key points:
    - all restrictions regarding the class and models of vehicle produced will be lifted within two years, leaving the car-maker free to make such decisions on a purely commercial basis;
    - provincial authorities alone will be able to approve investments in the sector up to $150 million (ceiling raised from $30 million), substantially reducing red tape for car manufacturers;
    - for the manufacture of engines, China's joint-venture requirement will be removed, allowing wholly foreign-owned production.

AGRICULTURE

- Market Access (Tariffs and Tariff Quotas): Improvements have been made on the tariffs on products such as rape oil (from 85% to 9%), pasta (from 25% to 15%), butter (from 30% to 10%), milk powder (from 25% to 10%), mandarins (from 40% to 12%), wine (from 65% to 14%), olives (from 25% to 10%) and wheat gluten (from 30% to 18%).
- Sanitary and Phytosanitary Measures: The EU and China signed an SPS Agreement that will provide for compliance by China with the WTO's SPS Agreement,

as well as resolving a number of bilateral SPS trade frictions. This agreement will be supplemented by subsequent agreements with individual EU Member States, to be concluded before China's formal entry into the WTO.

SERVICES

*   Telecommunications: The telecommunications offer has been considerably enhanced. China will open its mobile telephony market two years ahead of schedule, which is a crucial change in this fast-developing industry. For the first time, foreign operators will be permitted to establish as of accession (with a 25% share). This will rise to 35% one year after accession and 49% three years after accession. China has agreed to allow operations between Chinese cities (where the biggest business is located, covering more than 75% of current traffic) and not to restrict them to activity within each city. The liberalization of domestic leased circuit services will allow joint-venture foreign telecom operators to create their own network (independent from the existing one) and sell their capacity to clients in China. The EU has also obtained provisions to allow more competitors in the international corporate communications market. This will notably enable user companies (usually large corporations) to obtain better rates and services. Finally, China and the EU have agreed to a satisfactory settlement concerning the mobile investments of EU telecommunication companies (France Telecom, Siemens/Deutsche Telekom and Telecom Italia) in the second Chinese carrier, China Unicom.

- Insurance: Seven new licenses, five for life and two for non-life business, will be immediately provided to EU companies, and two more companies will be able to establish in another city (sub-branches). This will substantially increase the EU presence in China, as only four firms are currently in the market. Effective management control has been negotiated for foreign participants in life-insurance joint ventures, through choice of partner, and a legal guarantee of freedom from any regulatory interference in privately negotiated contracts, on a 50-50 equity basis. Foreign insurers will see their scope of business advanced by two years in life and non-life activities, selling the same products as their Chinese competitors. This includes health, pension and group insurance in life, and all non-life activities except for statutory insurance. Geographically, access of foreign insurers to Shenzen and Foshan has also been accelerated. Brokers (insurance intermediaries) will have access to the Chinese market through cross-border and local establishment for the first time. Upon accession, they will be able to establish on a 50-50 equity basis (with effective management control as indicated above). Foreign majority will be allowed within three years, and within five years there will be no equity restrictions. They will be able to undertake large-scale commercial risk and reinsurance business, which is the bulk of the brokerage market.
- Distribution: China has agreed to lift the specific 50-50 joint-venture restriction applicable to large retail stores (removing the 20,000 square meter size limit), as well as that for virtually all retail operations with more

than 30 outlets in China. Until now, if a retailer had wished to open more than 30 outlets, a 50-50 equity limit was applicable. In a country the size of China, this was obviously a very restrictive provision.

- Banking: The banking offer has also been improved. Distributors and other non-financial institutions will be able to give credit facilities for the purchase of all motor vehicles, rather than just cars. China has also agreed to allow foreign banks in the city of Zhuhai to advance their operations in local currency. Zhuhai, which is just off Macau, holds several EU banks.

- Securities: China and the EU have agreed to establish a regulatory dialogue on the development of the securities market in China. The EU welcomes the opportunity to contribute its expertise to the expansion of the Chinese securities market.

- Dredging: On accession, dredging activities related to infrastructure construction are open to foreign firms.

- Tourism: The tourism offer has been extended from holiday services to also cover corporate travel business. The establishment requirements for travel agencies and tour operators have been eased to the benefit, in particular, of SMEs (small and medium-sized enterprises) specialized in the Chinese market. The capital requirement will be gradually reduced to the same level as that applied to Chinese firms. The minimum turnover requirement has also been further reduced by 20% (down to $40 million).

- Construction: The joint-venture requirement has been relaxed to allow foreign majority on accession. Within three years, wholly foreign-owned enterprises will be permitted to carry out projects financed by foreigners (including those funded by the IMF, World Bank etc.) and Chinese-funded projects where Chinese construction firms justify the need for international assistance.

- Legal Services: Foreign law firms will be able, for the first time, to offer services on Chinese law. In particular they will be able to provide information to their clients on the Chinese legal environment. Concerning other activities in Chinese law (representations before the courts etc.), the arrangements with local law firms have been improved by allowing foreign firms directly to instruct individual Chinese lawyers in these firms. This will allow foreign firms to create a direct link with a Chinese lawyer of their choice, which may in practice be equivalent to full employment. Improvements have also been obtained on the prior experience requirements for lawyers — prior experience will no longer have to be consecutive, and the requirement for all lawyers, other than the chief representative, has been reduced from three to two years. Finally, it has been recognized for the first time that solicitors (although not members of a bar) will also be covered by the agreement.

- Accountancy: Accountants will be able to provide taxation and management consultancy services under the same conditions as accounting services, and will no longer be required to partner.

- Architects: Architects will now have an extended access on a cross-border basis, by allowing them to provide scheme design services.

- Market Research: The Chinese Decree imposing extremely burdensome requirements that might affect the confidentiality of market research reports will be substantially amended. Reports will no longer be pre-examined by Chinese authorities before being given to the client, but firms will merely have to send copies of questionnaires (not of the replies and results) to the authorities.

- Grandfathering: Protection of existing EU investments has been assured, even where they are on terms which exceed those available after China's accession.

HORIZONTAL ISSUES

- Government Procurement: China has agreed to full transparency and non-discrimination (MFN) in government purchases.
- Trade-distorting Investment-related Measures: The EU and China have agreed on commitments similar to those included in the Sino-US agreement, but also incorporating an obligation to eliminate industrial export subsidies, and offset requirements in the civil aircraft sector.
- National Treatment: This is a basic GATT obligation. China has now given specific commitments to phase out legislation that gives unfair advantages to domestic producers in the field of pharmaceutical pricing, after-sales services of imported goods, chemical-import registration requirements, control of imported boilers, and retail of imported cigarettes and spirits. In some cases, China will have one or two years to make her legislation WTO-compliant.

Source: European Union summary of the agreement. Downloaded from www.europa.eu.int/comm/trade/bilateral/china/res.pdf

Acronyms and Abbreviations

AFTA: ASEAN Free-Trade Area (*see also* ASEAN)
Intended to allow for duty-free access between all ASEAN members of goods produced in the region by 2005. The proposal has been set back by Malaysia's refusal to allow the inclusion of the automobile sector.

APEC: Asia-Pacific Economic Cooperation Forum
Its members include most Asian nations, the United States, Mexico, Australia, New Zealand and Chile. In 1994, members agreed to have a free-trade zone by 2010, for developed countries, and by 2020 for developing countries. In fact, there has been little progress toward that goal. APEC, instead, has evolved into little more than a talk shop, a useful place in which leaders (including, usually, the US President) can meet at annual summits.

ASEAN: Association of Southeast Asian Nations
Founded with US backing in 1967 as an anti-communist bulwark, its original members were Indonesia, Malaysia, the Philippines, Singapore and Thailand. Brunei joined in 1984. In the late 1990s, ASEAN expanded to include Burma, Cambodia, Laos and Vietnam.

ATC: WTO Agreement on Textiles and Clothing (*see also* MFA)

DSB: Dispute Settlement Body
This adjudicatory panel decides the rights and wrongs of trade disputes. It can order countries that are in violation of WTO procedures to take appropriate remedial action (though it cannot order specific remedies). If compliance isn't forthcoming within a reasonable period of time, the Body empowers countries that have been wronged to impose appropriate sanctions. The Body represents one of the biggest differences between the WTO and GATT.

GATT: General Agreement on Tariffs and Trade
Founded in 1947, GATT was a compromise institution set up after the US objected to a proposed International Trade Organization. Post-war planners were determined that the vicious cycle of trade and protectionism that occurred in the 1930s and helped precipitate World War II would never occur again. GATT was a multilateral organization dedicated to the principle that tariff and non-tariff barriers couldn't be raised arbitrarily and that no nation in the group should favor one member over another (the so-called Most Favored Nation status).

IMF: International Monetary Fund
Founded in 1946, this 183-member body is best-known for its emergency financial assistance to countries with an eye to rehabilitating their economies. Following a series of financial crises since the mid-1990s, the IMF has been going through a period of introspection and re-appraisal.

MFA: Multi-Fiber Arrangement
This provides for tough restrictions (including quotas) on clothing exports; it exists primarily to protect jobs in more-developed countries. The MFA was replaced by the WTO Agreement on Textiles and Clothing (ATC). The ATC will be phased out during a 10-year period ending on December 31, 2004. Developing countries oppose MFA because it makes it difficult to use the advantage of lower labor costs. It's a particularly distorting trade measure because the quota system gives producers incentives to produce in countries where it wouldn't otherwise be economical. China will be one of the biggest, if not the biggest, beneficiary of MFA's elimination. However, the US-China bilateral accord allows the US to keep ATC-style restrictions in place for another four years, until December 31, 2008.

MFN: Most Favored Nation status (*see* NTR)

MOFTEC: Ministry of Foreign Trade and Economic Cooperation
China's ministry responsible for WTO negotiations. The current minister is Shi Guangsheng. His predecessor, until she was promoted to be a State Councillor in 1998, was Wu Yi.

NTR: Normal Trading Relations
This prohibits discrimination against fellow WTO members and replaces the old MFN arrangement under GATT. Because China wasn't a WTO member, the US could threaten to withdraw its MFN or NTR status, as it did following the Tiananmen Square crackdown in 1989. The annual MFN/NTR debates became the primary forum in

the United States where opponents of China could voice their unhappiness with Beijing. The US accorded China Permanent NTR, or PNTR, upon accession.

QUAD: An influential trade grouping consisting of Canada, the European Union, Japan and the United States
The QUAD plays a leading role in trade negotiations, because of its economic dominance. However, developing countries have bristled at the QUAD's traditional role of setting the agenda for trade negotiations and thus have undermined the rich-country group's primacy in recent years. Calls for greater transparency at the WTO partly reflect unhappiness with the QUAD's power. China's WTO accession is expected to further dilute the QUAD's influence.

S&D: Special and differential treatment
This is a clause designed to provide extra assistance for developing countries. This became a contentious issue for China, which insisted that it wanted to join as a developing country. The US worried that China's impact on trade would be disruptive and so refused to concede on full S&D treatment. The final sticking point was agriculture. The US wanted to cap China's subsidies at 5% of the production value, while China fought for 10%. The two sides settled on a compromise level of 8.5%.

TBT: Agreement on Technical Barriers to Trade
The TBT prohibits the use of tests and standards as a way of discriminating unjustly against trading partners or protecting domestic industries. The TBT encourages the

use of internationally recognized tests wherever possible. A related agreement, the Sanitary and Phytosanitary Standards agreement, covers food and agricultural areas.

TRIMs: Trade-Related Investment Measures
This agreement, concluded during the Uruguay Round (see below), is primarily aimed at prohibiting developing countries from using market-distorting measures such as local-content requirements. Developing countries already in the WTO were given until December 31, 1999 to phase out five specific TRIMs that were illegal under GATT. Besides a ban on local-content requirements, countries are no longer allowed to insist on trade-balancing requirements (where imports must be offset by exports), foreign-exchange balance requirements (a similar measure, but focused on the amount of foreign exchange needed), foreign-exchange restrictions and restrictions on domestic sales in order to encourage exports.

TRIPs: Trade-Related Aspects of Intellectual-Property Rights
TRIPs covers copyrights, trademarks, patents, industrial designs and the like. It was negotiated during the Uruguay Round at the urging of the developed countries, who were frustrated at piracy of everything from pharmaceuticals to computer software to semiconductor designs. Areas such as these patents have become a major bone of contention between the developed and developing world. Developing countries could enjoy a five-year grace period, which ended on January 1, 2000; least-developed countries have until 2005. New WTO members must comply upon accession.

UR: Uruguay Round
Delegates at a meeting in Punta del Este, Uruguay, in 1986 agreed to launch a new round of trade talks. The talks, which had been proposed as early as 1982, formally began in 1987. The talks, which weren't completed until 1994, resulted in the establishment of the WTO. A major achievement of the Uruguay Round was to make agriculture subject to the discipline of the GATT regime. When GATT was founded in 1947, it treated agriculture differently from manufactures; both quotas and export subsidies were allowed for farm products. For the first time, services were also included in the UR negotiations. The resulting accord covering services was the General Agreement on Trade in Services.

USTR: United States Trade Representative
The cabinet-level officer responsible for trade negotiations and policy. Robert Zoellick is George W. Bush's USTR; his predecessor was Charlene Barshefsky. The USTR heads the Office of the United States Trade Representative. "USTR" commonly is used to refer to both the Ambassador and the Office.

WTO: World Trade Organization
The WTO provides the legal and institutional foundation for the new multilateral trading system that came into being on January 1, 1995. It replaced the General Agreement on Tariffs and Trade (GATT). The biggest difference between the two was the dispute settlement body (DSB), which acted as a court to adjudicate trade disputes. This gives the WTO disciplinary power of a sort that GATT didn't have.

Index